While *The Bluecoats* is clearly not a history book, it is a series that tends to root itself in actual historical facts. For example, the *David* really did exist and worked along the principles explained in this story.

Perhaps it is worth pointing out, however, that the real *David* and its sister ships were a lot less effective than shown here. We heartily encourage you to read up on their story; while not nearly as hilarious as this version, it is a fascinating one in terms of ingenuity and dogged courage.

Original title: Les Tuniques Bleues – Le David
Original edition: © Dupuis, 1982
by Lambil & Cauvin
www.dupuis.com
All rights reserved
English translation: © 2019 Cinebook Ltd
Translator: Jerome Saincantin
Editor: Erica Olson Jeffrey
Lettering and text layout: Design Amorandi
Printed in Spain by EGEDSA
This edition first published in Great Britain in 2019 by
Cinebook Ltd
56 Beech Avenue
Canterbury, Kent
CT4 7TA
www.cinebook.com
A CIP catalogue record for this book
is available from the British Library
ISBN 978-1-84918-430-4

9th CINEBOOK
The 9th Art Publisher

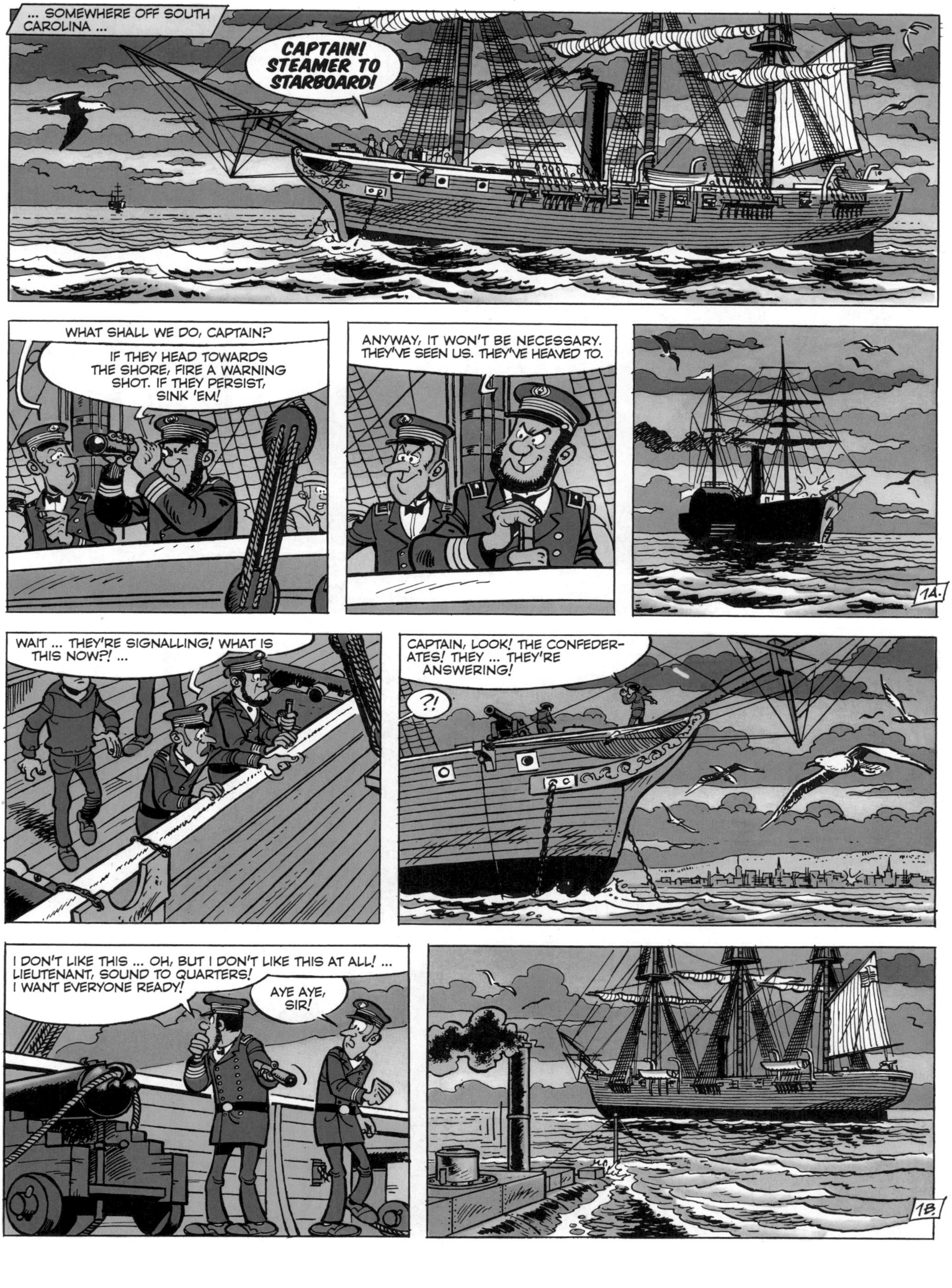
... SOMEWHERE OFF SOUTH CAROLINA ...
CAPTAIN! STEAMER TO STARBOARD!
WHAT SHALL WE DO, CAPTAIN?
IF THEY HEAD TOWARDS THE SHORE, FIRE A WARNING SHOT. IF THEY PERSIST, SINK 'EM!
ANYWAY, IT WON'T BE NECESSARY. THEY'VE SEEN US. THEY'VE HEAVED TO.
1A.
WAIT ... THEY'RE SIGNALLING! WHAT IS THIS NOW?! ...
CAPTAIN, LOOK! THE CONFEDERATES! THEY ... THEY'RE ANSWERING!
?!
I DON'T LIKE THIS ... OH, BUT I DON'T LIKE THIS AT ALL! ... LIEUTENANT, SOUND TO QUARTERS! I WANT EVERYONE READY!
AYE AYE, SIR!
1B.

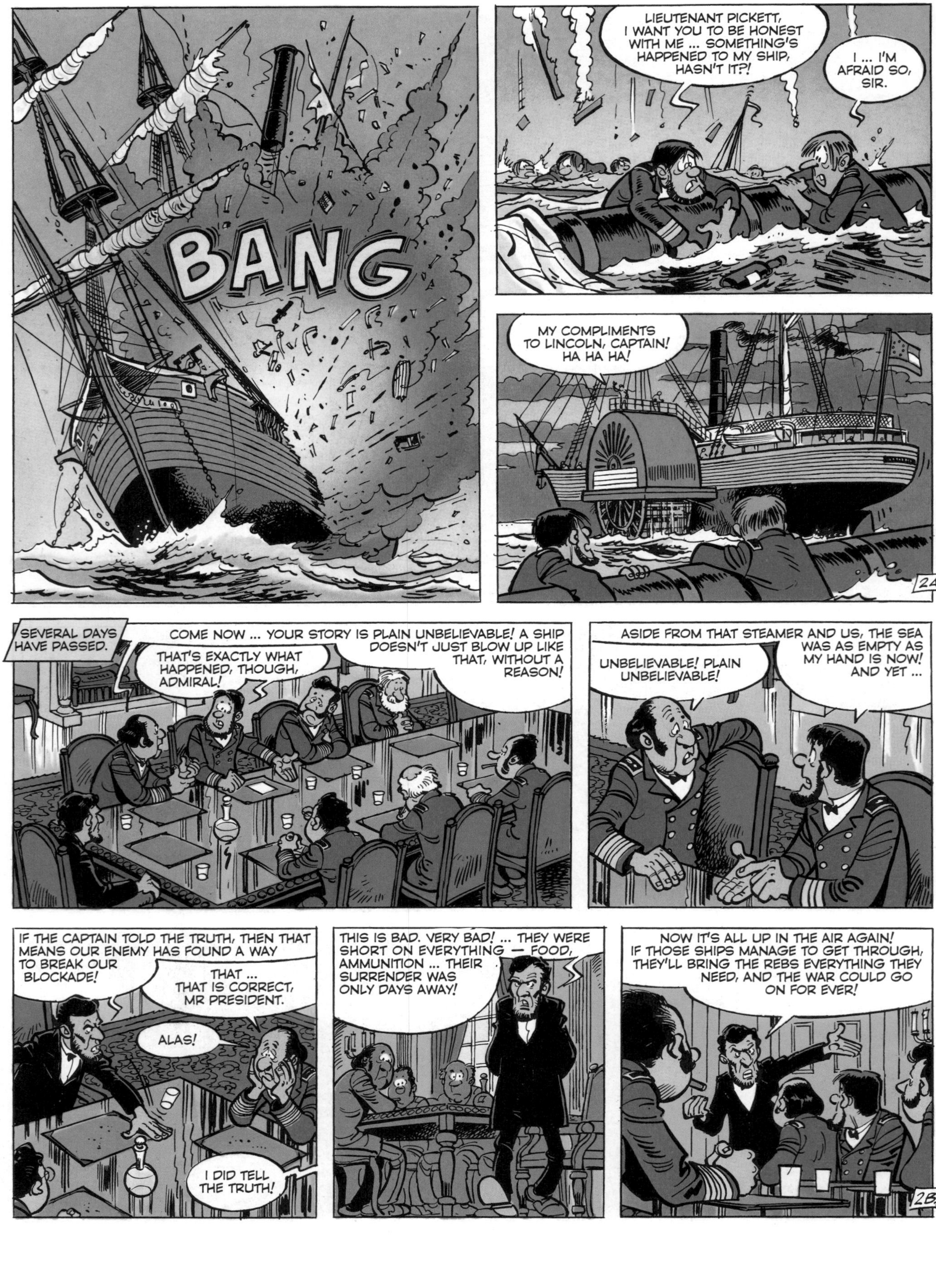
BANG
LIEUTENANT PICKETT, I WANT YOU TO BE HONEST WITH ME ... SOMETHING'S HAPPENED TO MY SHIP, HASN'T IT?!
I ... I'M AFRAID SO, SIR.
MY COMPLIMENTS TO LINCOLN, CAPTAIN! HA HA HA!
2A.
SEVERAL DAYS HAVE PASSED.
COME NOW ... YOUR STORY IS PLAIN UNBELIEVABLE! A SHIP DOESN'T JUST BLOW UP LIKE THAT, WITHOUT A REASON!
THAT'S EXACTLY WHAT HAPPENED, THOUGH, ADMIRAL!
ASIDE FROM THAT STEAMER AND US, THE SEA WAS AS EMPTY AS MY HAND IS NOW! AND YET ...
UNBELIEVABLE! PLAIN UNBELIEVABLE!
IF THE CAPTAIN TOLD THE TRUTH, THEN THAT MEANS OUR ENEMY HAS FOUND A WAY TO BREAK OUR BLOCKADE!
THAT ... THAT IS CORRECT, MR PRESIDENT.
ALAS!
I DID TELL THE TRUTH!
THIS IS BAD. VERY BAD! ... THEY WERE SHORT ON EVERYTHING — FOOD, AMMUNITION ... THEIR SURRENDER WAS ONLY DAYS AWAY!
NOW IT'S ALL UP IN THE AIR AGAIN! IF THOSE SHIPS MANAGE TO GET THROUGH, THEY'LL BRING THE REBS EVERYTHING THEY NEED, AND THE WAR COULD GO ON FOR EVER!
2B.

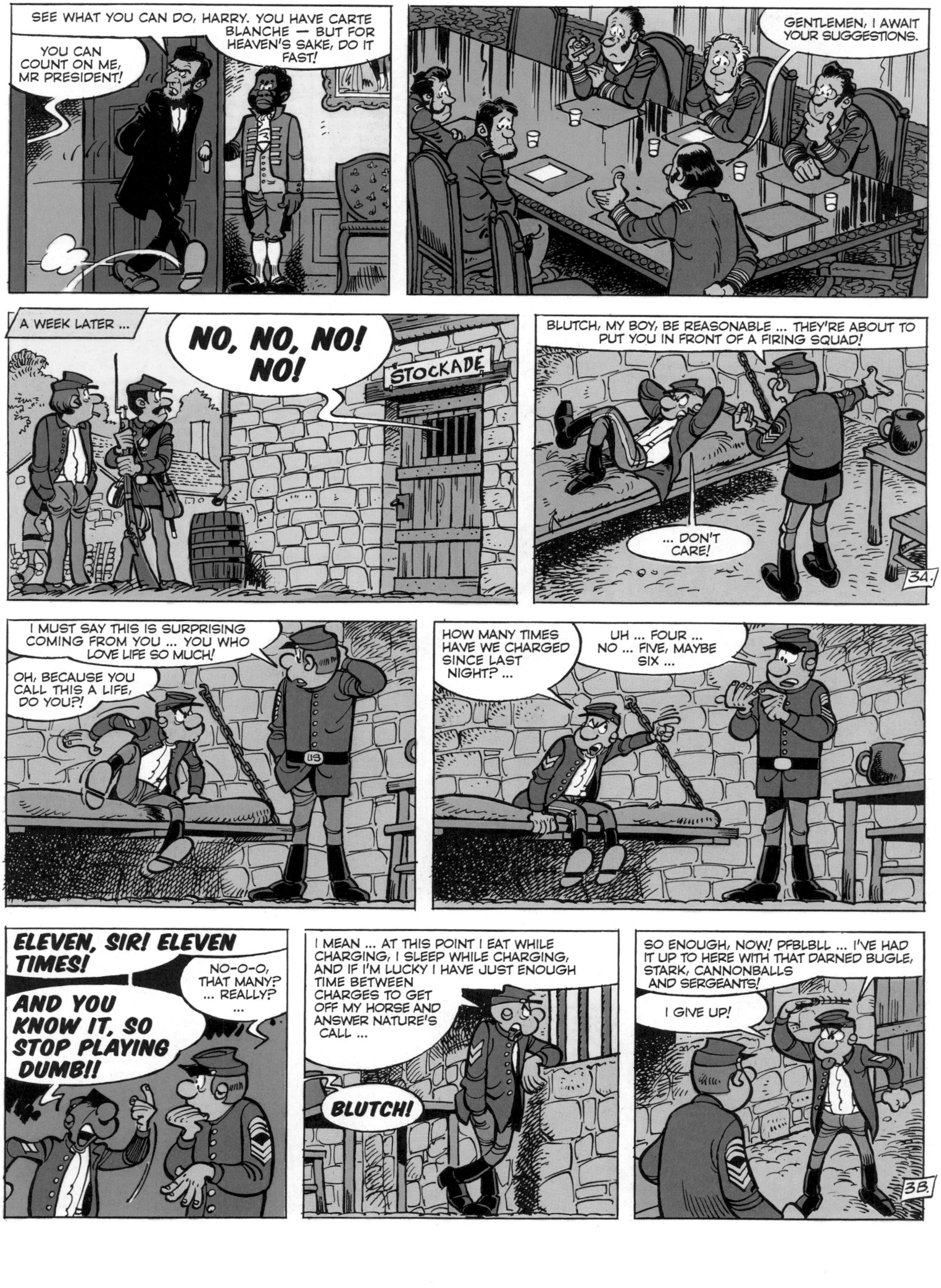
SEE WHAT YOU CAN DO, HARRY. YOU HAVE CARTE BLANCHE — BUT FOR HEAVEN'S SAKE, DO IT FAST!
YOU CAN COUNT ON ME, MR PRESIDENT!
GENTLEMEN, I AWAIT YOUR SUGGESTIONS.
A WEEK LATER ...
NO, NO, NO! NO!
STOCKADE
BLUTCH, MY BOY, BE REASONABLE ... THEY'RE ABOUT TO PUT YOU IN FRONT OF A FIRING SQUAD!
... DON'T CARE!
I MUST SAY THIS IS SURPRISING COMING FROM YOU ... YOU WHO LOVE LIFE SO MUCH!
OH, BECAUSE YOU CALL THIS A LIFE, DO YOU?!
HOW MANY TIMES HAVE WE CHARGED SINCE LAST NIGHT? ...
UH ... FOUR ... NO ... FIVE, MAYBE SIX ...
ELEVEN, SIR! ELEVEN TIMES!
NO-O-O, THAT MANY? ... REALLY? ...
AND YOU KNOW IT, SO STOP PLAYING DUMB!!
I MEAN ... AT THIS POINT I EAT WHILE CHARGING, I SLEEP WHILE CHARGING, AND IF I'M LUCKY I HAVE JUST ENOUGH TIME BETWEEN CHARGES TO GET OFF MY HORSE AND ANSWER NATURE'S CALL ...
BLUTCH!
SO ENOUGH, NOW! PFBLBLL ... I'VE HAD IT UP TO HERE WITH THAT DARNED BUGLE, STARK, CANNONBALLS AND SERGEANTS!
I GIVE UP!

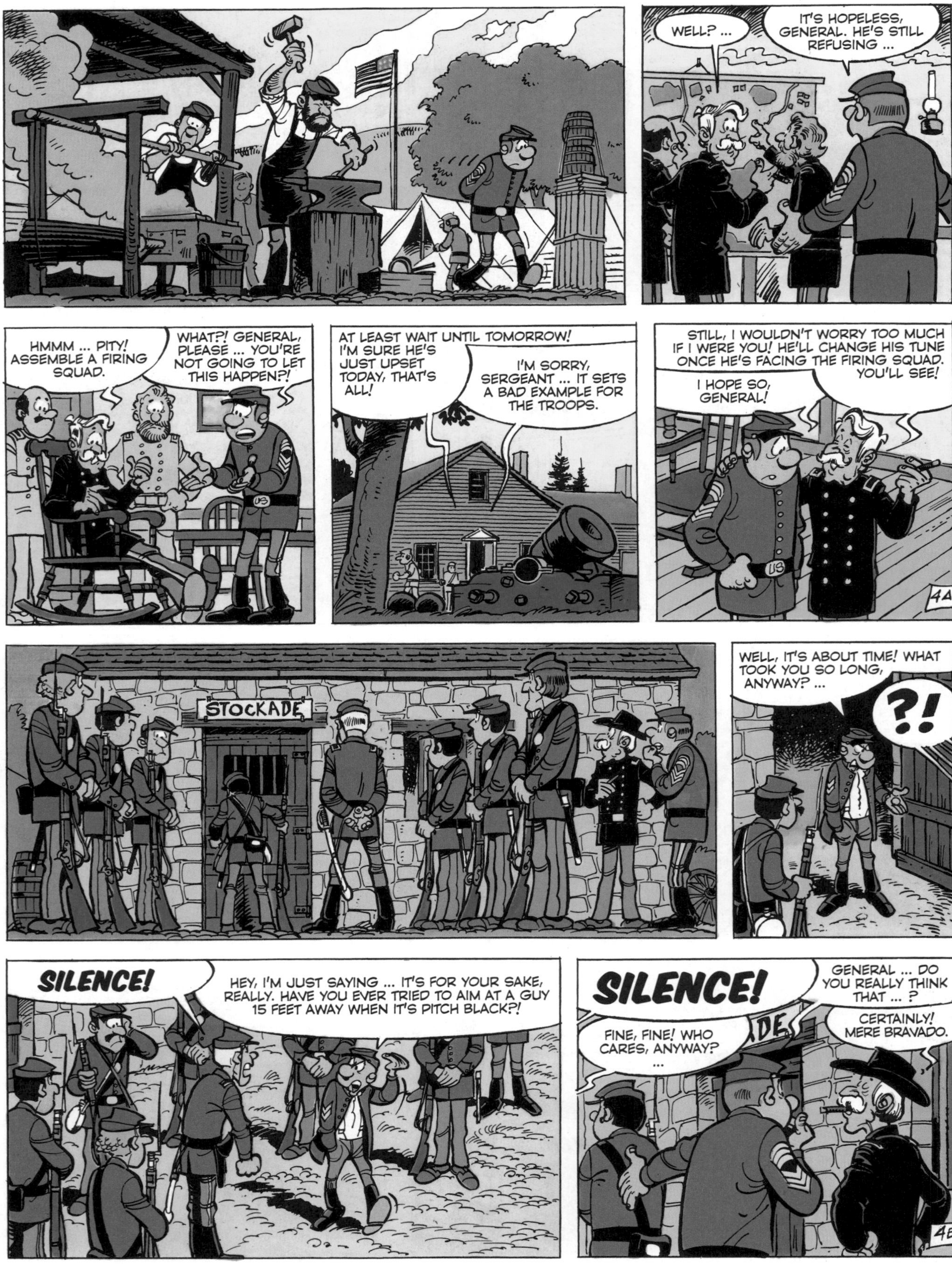
WELL? ...
IT'S HOPELESS, GENERAL. HE'S STILL REFUSING ...
HMMM ... PITY! ASSEMBLE A FIRING SQUAD.
WHAT?! GENERAL, PLEASE ... YOU'RE NOT GOING TO LET THIS HAPPEN?!
AT LEAST WAIT UNTIL TOMORROW! I'M SURE HE'S JUST UPSET TODAY, THAT'S ALL!
I'M SORRY, SERGEANT ... IT SETS A BAD EXAMPLE FOR THE TROOPS.
STILL, I WOULDN'T WORRY TOO MUCH IF I WERE YOU! HE'LL CHANGE HIS TUNE ONCE HE'S FACING THE FIRING SQUAD. YOU'LL SEE!
I HOPE SO, GENERAL!
4A.
STOCKADE
WELL, IT'S ABOUT TIME! WHAT TOOK YOU SO LONG, ANYWAY? ...
?!
SILENCE!
HEY, I'M JUST SAYING ... IT'S FOR YOUR SAKE, REALLY. HAVE YOU EVER TRIED TO AIM AT A GUY 15 FEET AWAY WHEN IT'S PITCH BLACK?!
SILENCE!
FINE, FINE! WHO CARES, ANYWAY? ...
GENERAL ... DO YOU REALLY THINK THAT ... ?
CERTAINLY! MERE BRAVADO.
4B.

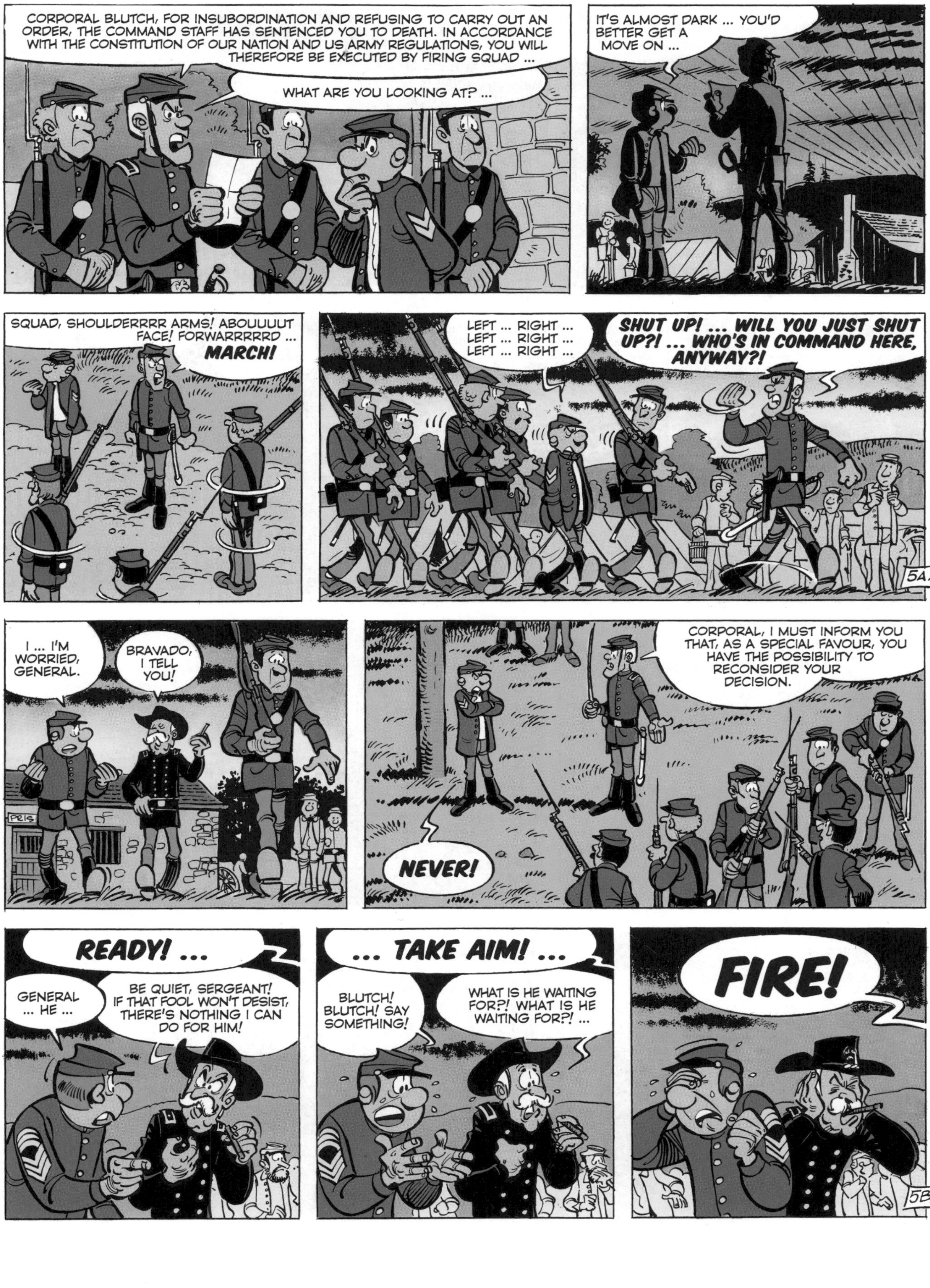
CORPORAL BLUTCH, FOR INSUBORDINATION AND REFUSING TO CARRY OUT AN ORDER, THE COMMAND STAFF HAS SENTENCED YOU TO DEATH. IN ACCORDANCE WITH THE CONSTITUTION OF OUR NATION AND US ARMY REGULATIONS, YOU WILL THEREFORE BE EXECUTED BY FIRING SQUAD ...
WHAT ARE YOU LOOKING AT? ...
IT'S ALMOST DARK ... YOU'D BETTER GET A MOVE ON ...
SQUAD, SHOULDERRRR ARMS! ABOUUUUT FACE! FORWARRRRRD ... MARCH!
LEFT ... RIGHT ... LEFT ... RIGHT ... LEFT ... RIGHT ...
SHUT UP! ... WILL YOU JUST SHUT UP?! ... WHO'S IN COMMAND HERE, ANYWAY?!
5A.
I ... I'M WORRIED, GENERAL.
BRAVADO, I TELL YOU!
PRIS
CORPORAL, I MUST INFORM YOU THAT, AS A SPECIAL FAVOUR, YOU HAVE THE POSSIBILITY TO RECONSIDER YOUR DECISION.
NEVER!
READY! ...
GENERAL ... HE ...
BE QUIET, SERGEANT! IF THAT FOOL WON'T DESIST, THERE'S NOTHING I CAN DO FOR HIM!
... TAKE AIM! ...
BLUTCH! BLUTCH! SAY SOMETHING!
WHAT IS HE WAITING FOR?! WHAT IS HE WAITING FOR?! ...
FIRE!
5B.

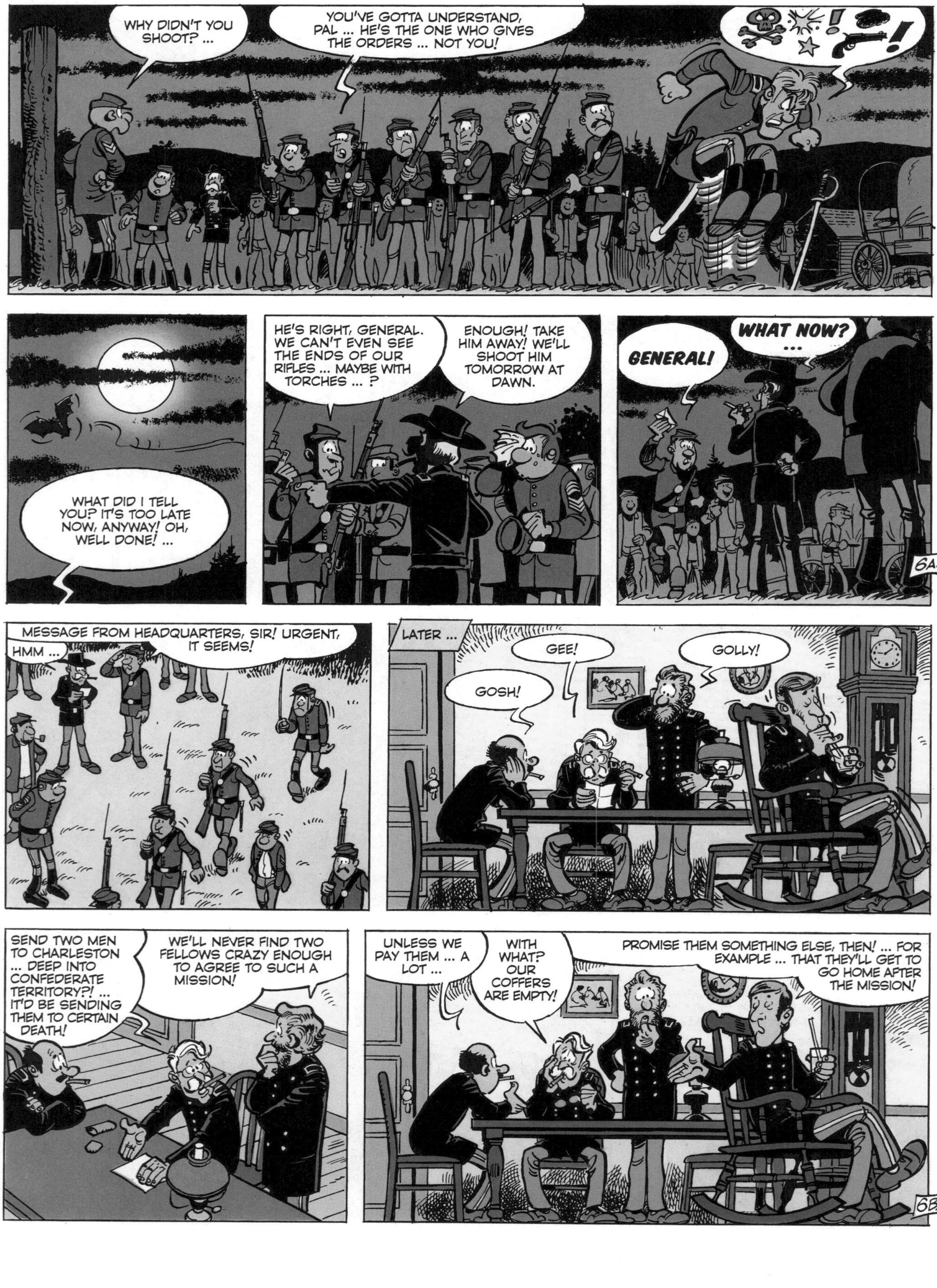

WHY DIDN'T YOU SHOOT? ...
YOU'VE GOTTA UNDERSTAND, PAL ... HE'S THE ONE WHO GIVES THE ORDERS ... NOT YOU!
!
!
WHAT DID I TELL YOU? IT'S TOO LATE NOW, ANYWAY! OH, WELL DONE! ...
HE'S RIGHT, GENERAL. WE CAN'T EVEN SEE THE ENDS OF OUR RIFLES ... MAYBE WITH TORCHES ... ?
ENOUGH! TAKE HIM AWAY! WE'LL SHOOT HIM TOMORROW AT DAWN.
GENERAL!
WHAT NOW? ...
MESSAGE FROM HEADQUARTERS, SIR! URGENT, IT SEEMS!
HMM ...
LATER ...
GOSH!
GEE!
GOLLY!
SEND TWO MEN TO CHARLESTON ... DEEP INTO CONFEDERATE TERRITORY?! ... IT'D BE SENDING THEM TO CERTAIN DEATH!
WE'LL NEVER FIND TWO FELLOWS CRAZY ENOUGH TO AGREE TO SUCH A MISSION!
UNLESS WE PAY THEM ... A LOT ...
WITH WHAT? OUR COFFERS ARE EMPTY!
PROMISE THEM SOMETHING ELSE, THEN! ... FOR EXAMPLE ... THAT THEY'LL GET TO GO HOME AFTER THE MISSION!

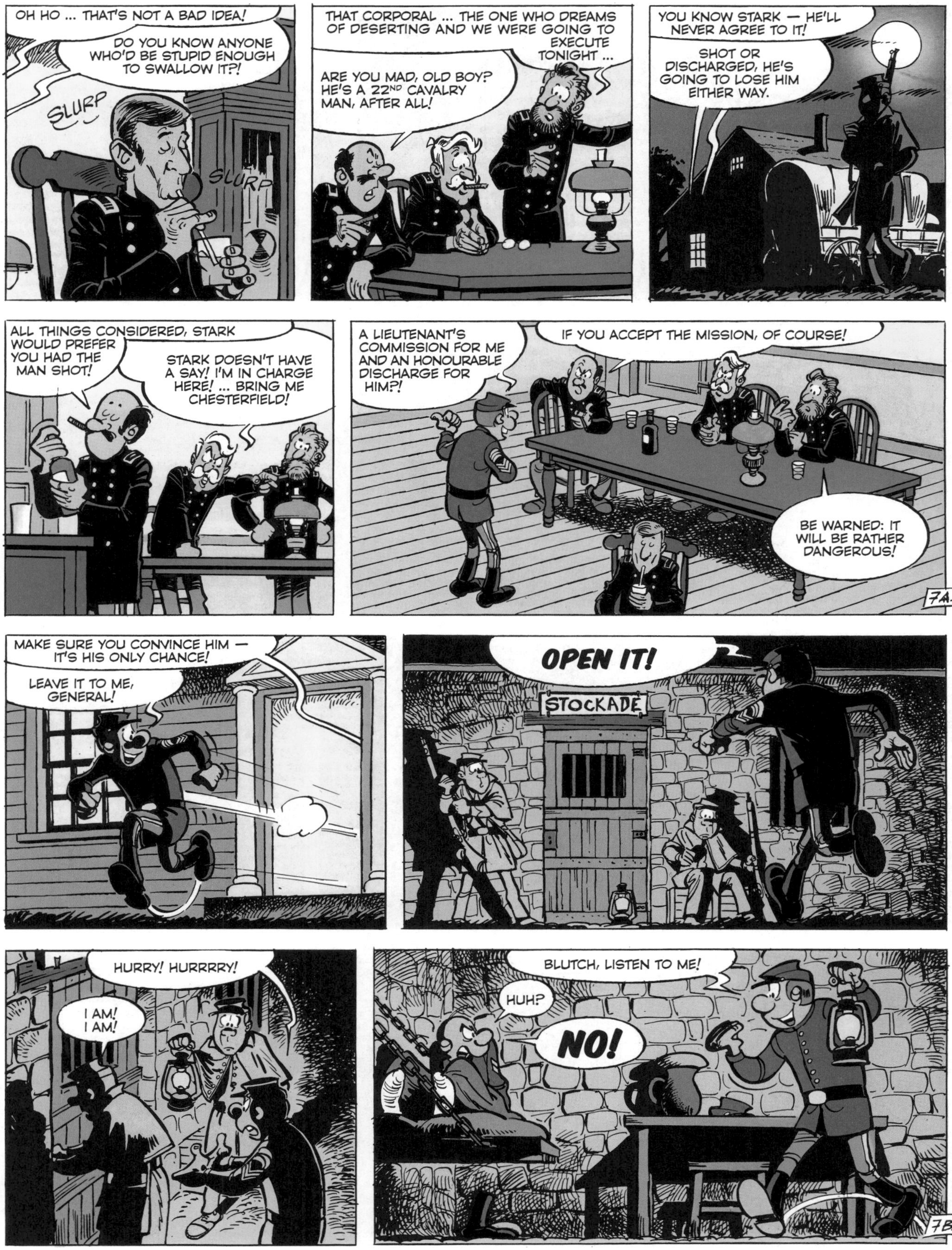

OH HO ... THAT'S NOT A BAD IDEA!
DO YOU KNOW ANYONE WHO'D BE STUPID ENOUGH TO SWALLOW IT?!
SLURP
SLURP
THAT CORPORAL ... THE ONE WHO DREAMS OF DESERTING AND WE WERE GOING TO EXECUTE TONIGHT ...
ARE YOU MAD, OLD BOY? HE'S A 22ND CAVALRY MAN, AFTER ALL!
YOU KNOW STARK — HE'LL NEVER AGREE TO IT!
SHOT OR DISCHARGED, HE'S GOING TO LOSE HIM EITHER WAY.
ALL THINGS CONSIDERED, STARK WOULD PREFER YOU HAD THE MAN SHOT!
STARK DOESN'T HAVE A SAY! I'M IN CHARGE HERE! ... BRING ME CHESTERFIELD!
A LIEUTENANT'S COMMISSION FOR ME AND AN HONOURABLE DISCHARGE FOR HIM?!
IF YOU ACCEPT THE MISSION, OF COURSE!
BE WARNED: IT WILL BE RATHER DANGEROUS!
7A.
MAKE SURE YOU CONVINCE HIM — IT'S HIS ONLY CHANCE!
LEAVE IT TO ME, GENERAL!
OPEN IT!
STOCKADE
HURRY! HURRRRY!
I AM! I AM!
BLUTCH, LISTEN TO ME!
HUH?
NO!
7B.

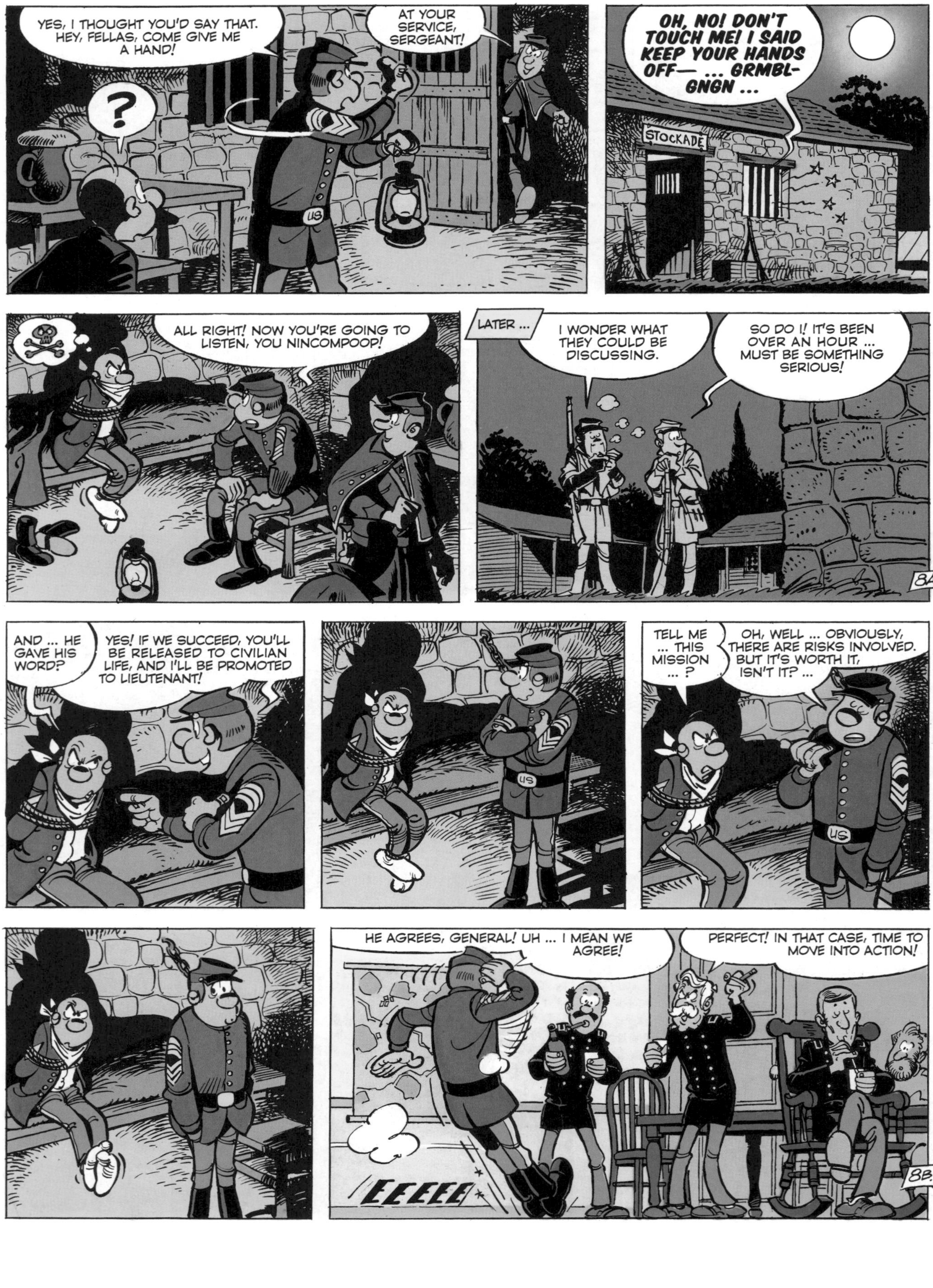
YES, I THOUGHT YOU'D SAY THAT. HEY, FELLAS, COME GIVE ME A HAND!
?
AT YOUR SERVICE, SERGEANT!
US
OH, NO! DON'T TOUCH ME! I SAID KEEP YOUR HANDS OFF— ... GRMBL-GNGN ...
STOCKADE
ALL RIGHT! NOW YOU'RE GOING TO LISTEN, YOU NINCOMPOOP!
LATER ...
I WONDER WHAT THEY COULD BE DISCUSSING.
SO DO I! IT'S BEEN OVER AN HOUR ... MUST BE SOMETHING SERIOUS!
8A
AND ... HE GAVE HIS WORD?
YES! IF WE SUCCEED, YOU'LL BE RELEASED TO CIVILIAN LIFE, AND I'LL BE PROMOTED TO LIEUTENANT!
US
TELL ME ... THIS MISSION ... ?
OH, WELL ... OBVIOUSLY, THERE ARE RISKS INVOLVED. BUT IT'S WORTH IT, ISN'T IT? ...
US
HE AGREES, GENERAL! UH ... I MEAN WE AGREE!
PERFECT! IN THAT CASE, TIME TO MOVE INTO ACTION!
EEEEE
8B

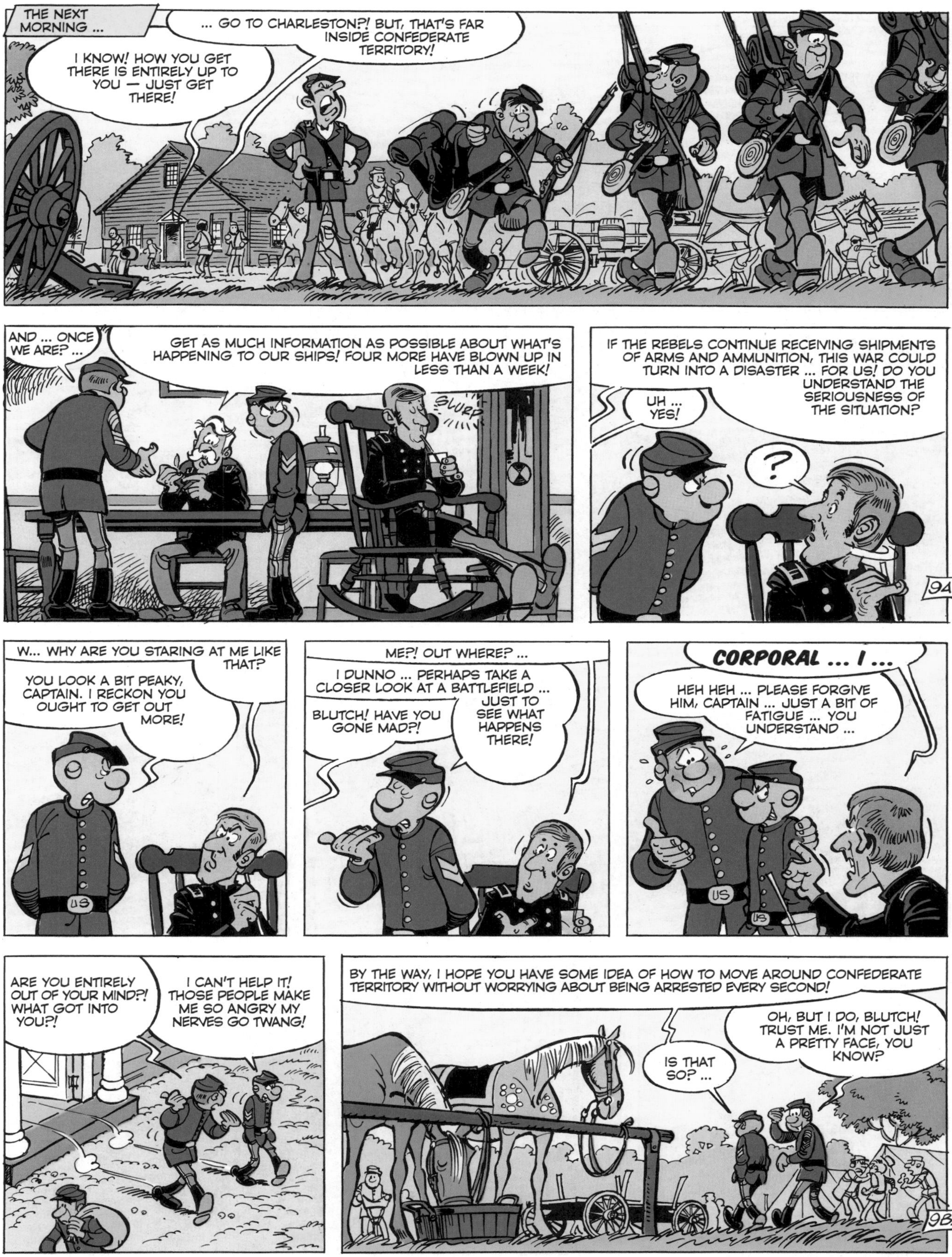

THE NEXT MORNING ...
... GO TO CHARLESTON?! BUT, THAT'S FAR INSIDE CONFEDERATE TERRITORY!
I KNOW! HOW YOU GET THERE IS ENTIRELY UP TO YOU — JUST GET THERE!
AND ... ONCE WE ARE? ...
GET AS MUCH INFORMATION AS POSSIBLE ABOUT WHAT'S HAPPENING TO OUR SHIPS! FOUR MORE HAVE BLOWN UP IN LESS THAN A WEEK!
SLURP
IF THE REBELS CONTINUE RECEIVING SHIPMENTS OF ARMS AND AMMUNITION, THIS WAR COULD TURN INTO A DISASTER ... FOR US! DO YOU UNDERSTAND THE SERIOUSNESS OF THE SITUATION?
UH ... YES!
?
9A.
W... WHY ARE YOU STARING AT ME LIKE THAT?
YOU LOOK A BIT PEAKY, CAPTAIN. I RECKON YOU OUGHT TO GET OUT MORE!
ME?! OUT WHERE? ...
I DUNNO ... PERHAPS TAKE A CLOSER LOOK AT A BATTLEFIELD ...
JUST TO SEE WHAT HAPPENS THERE!
BLUTCH! HAVE YOU GONE MAD?!
CORPORAL ... I ...
HEH HEH ... PLEASE FORGIVE HIM, CAPTAIN ... JUST A BIT OF FATIGUE ... YOU UNDERSTAND ...
ARE YOU ENTIRELY OUT OF YOUR MIND?! WHAT GOT INTO YOU?!
I CAN'T HELP IT! THOSE PEOPLE MAKE ME SO ANGRY MY NERVES GO TWANG!
BY THE WAY, I HOPE YOU HAVE SOME IDEA OF HOW TO MOVE AROUND CONFEDERATE TERRITORY WITHOUT WORRYING ABOUT BEING ARRESTED EVERY SECOND!
IS THAT SO? ...
OH, BUT I DO, BLUTCH! TRUST ME. I'M NOT JUST A PRETTY FACE, YOU KNOW?
9B.

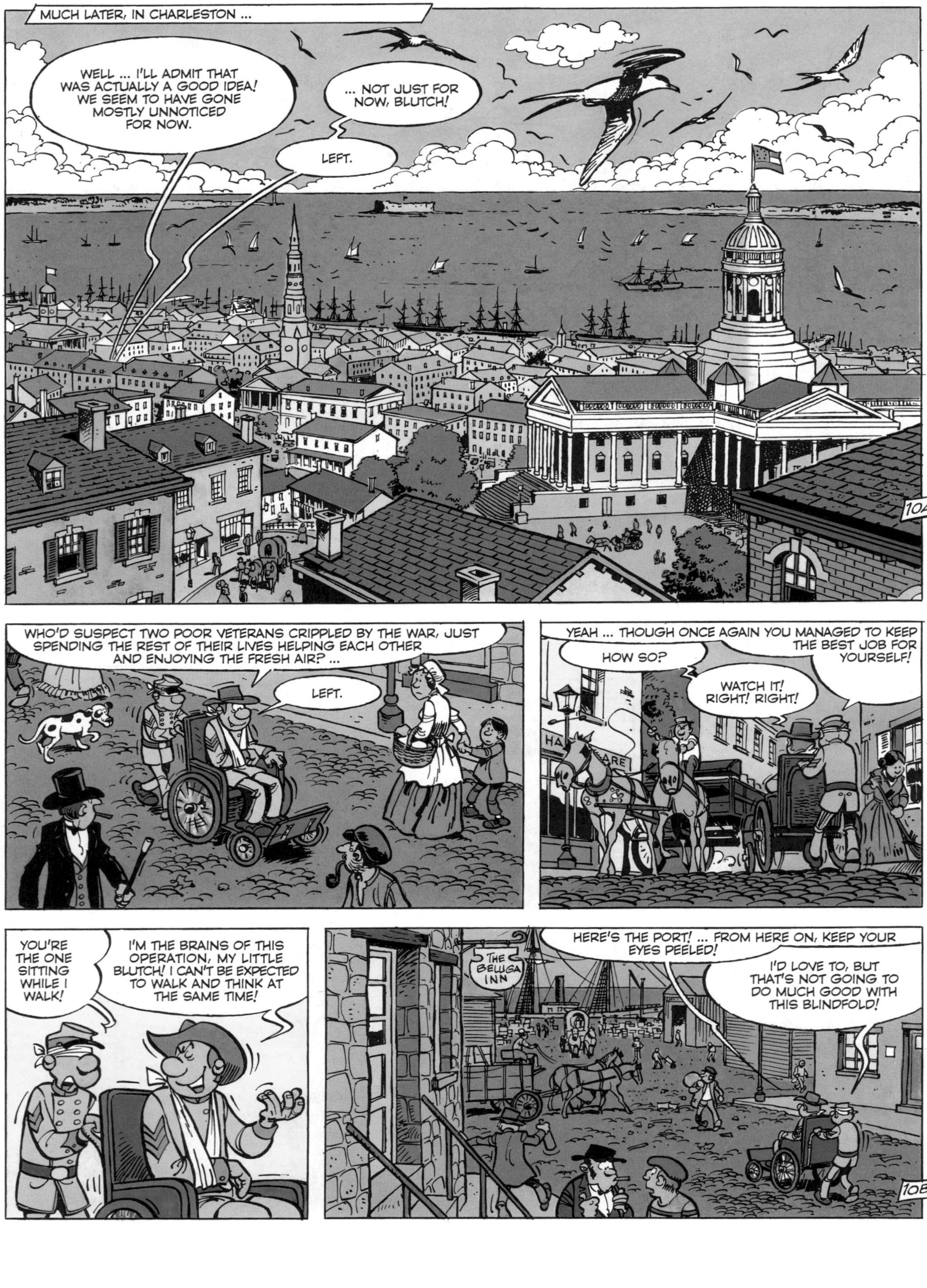
MUCH LATER, IN CHARLESTON ...
WELL ... I'LL ADMIT THAT WAS ACTUALLY A GOOD IDEA! WE SEEM TO HAVE GONE MOSTLY UNNOTICED FOR NOW.
... NOT JUST FOR NOW, BLUTCH!
LEFT.
10A
WHO'D SUSPECT TWO POOR VETERANS CRIPPLED BY THE WAR, JUST SPENDING THE REST OF THEIR LIVES HELPING EACH OTHER AND ENJOYING THE FRESH AIR? ...
LEFT.
YEAH ... THOUGH ONCE AGAIN YOU MANAGED TO KEEP THE BEST JOB FOR YOURSELF!
HOW SO?
WATCH IT! RIGHT! RIGHT!
YOU'RE THE ONE SITTING WHILE I WALK!
I'M THE BRAINS OF THIS OPERATION, MY LITTLE BLUTCH! I CAN'T BE EXPECTED TO WALK AND THINK AT THE SAME TIME!
THE BELUGA INN
HERE'S THE PORT! ... FROM HERE ON, KEEP YOUR EYES PEELED!
I'D LOVE TO, BUT THAT'S NOT GOING TO DO MUCH GOOD WITH THIS BLINDFOLD!
10B

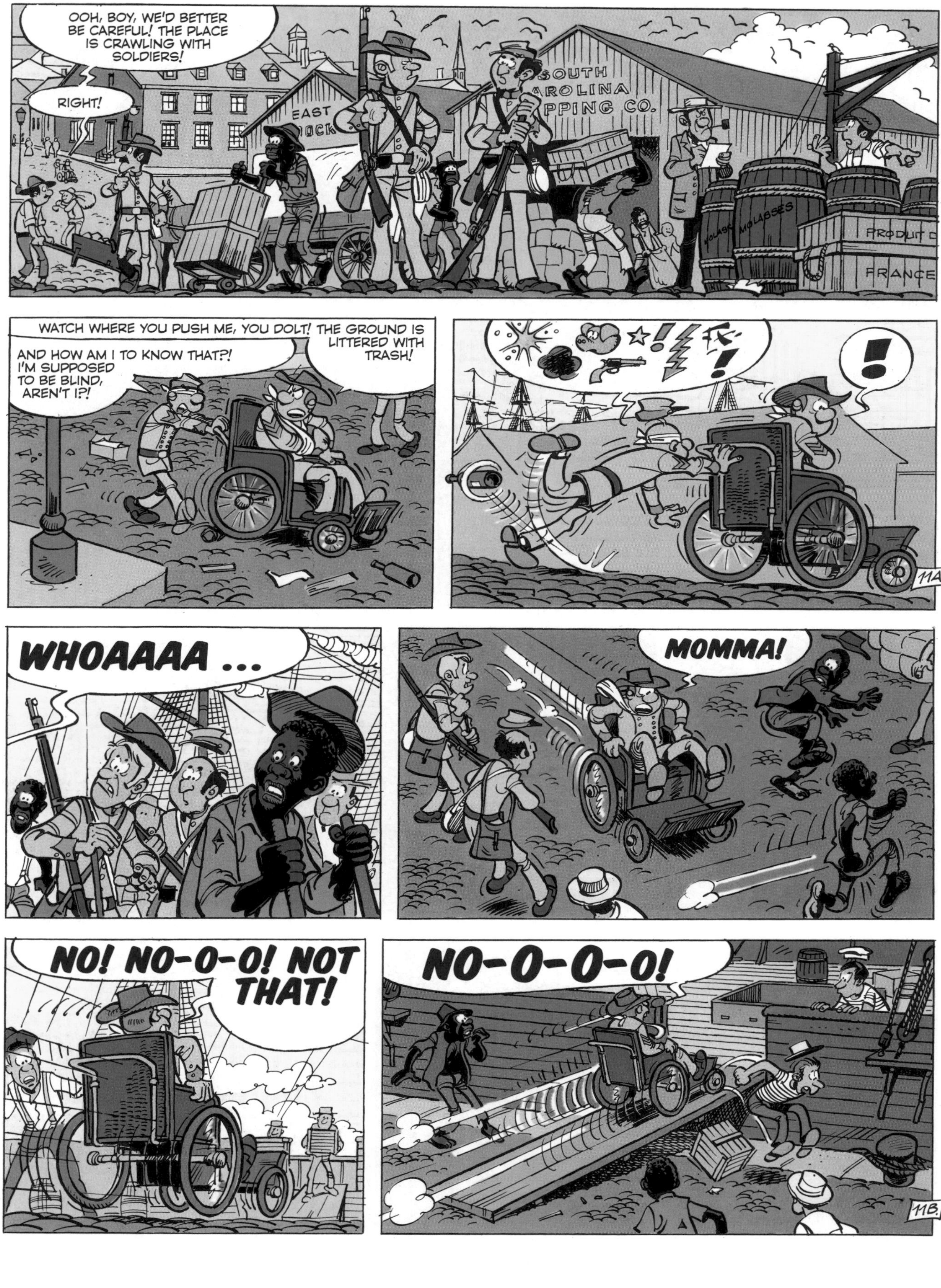
OOH, BOY, WE'D BETTER BE CAREFUL! THE PLACE IS CRAWLING WITH SOLDIERS!
RIGHT!
EAST
SOUTH
MOLASSES
FRANCE
WATCH WHERE YOU PUSH ME, YOU DOLT! THE GROUND IS LITTERED WITH TRASH!
AND HOW AM I TO KNOW THAT?! I'M SUPPOSED TO BE BLIND, AREN'T I?!
!
11A
WHOAAAA ...
MOMMA!
NO! NO-O-O! NOT THAT!
NO-O-O-O!
11B

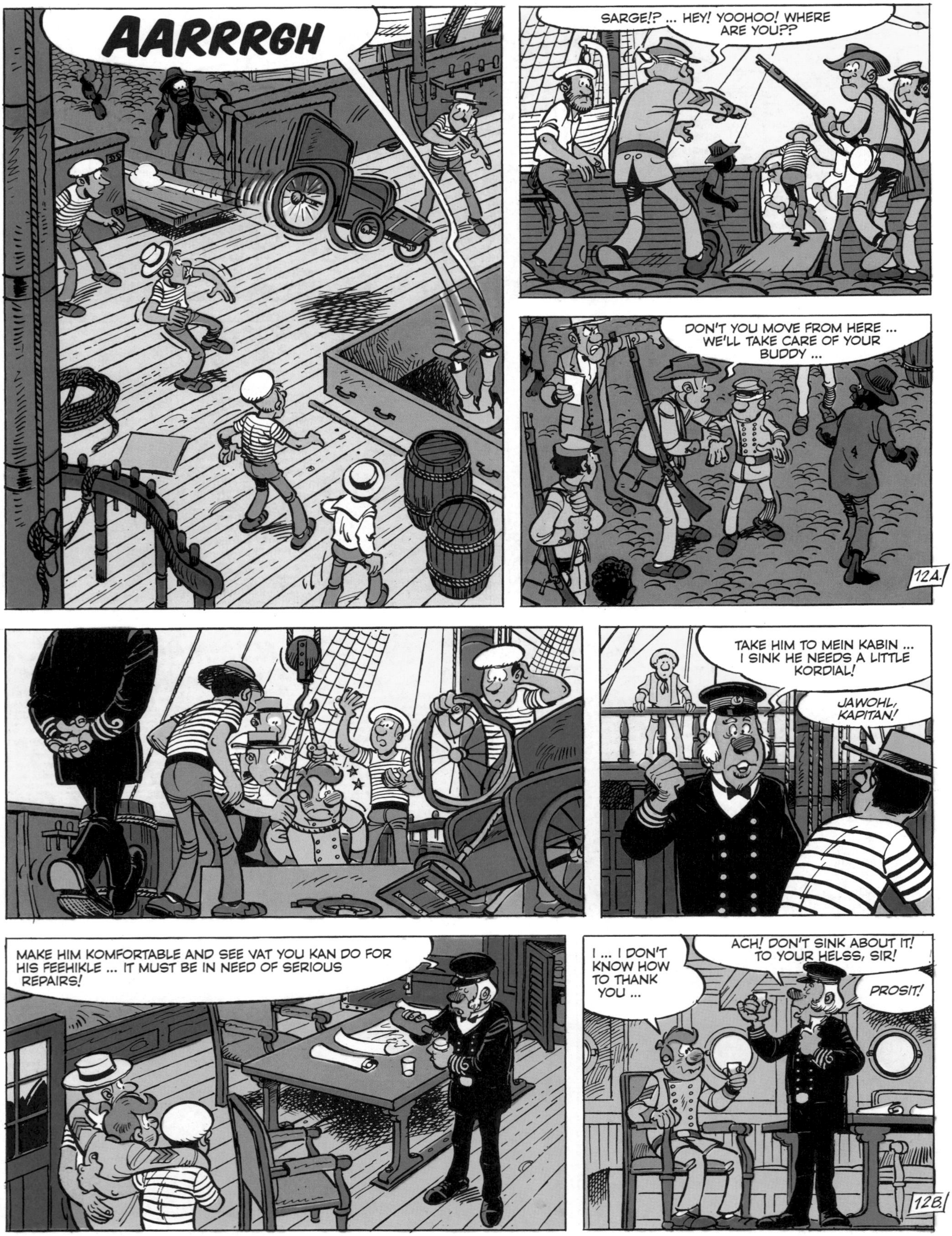
AARRRGH
SARGE!? ... HEY! YOOHOO! WHERE ARE YOU??
DON'T YOU MOVE FROM HERE ... WE'LL TAKE CARE OF YOUR BUDDY ...
12A
TAKE HIM TO MEIN KABIN ... I SINK HE NEEDS A LITTLE KORDIAL!
JAWOHL, KAPITAN!
MAKE HIM KOMFORTABLE AND SEE VAT YOU KAN DO FOR HIS FEEHIKLE ... IT MUST BE IN NEED OF SERIOUS REPAIRS!
I ... I DON'T KNOW HOW TO THANK YOU ...
ACH! DON'T SINK ABOUT IT! TO YOUR HELSS, SIR!
PROSIT!
12B

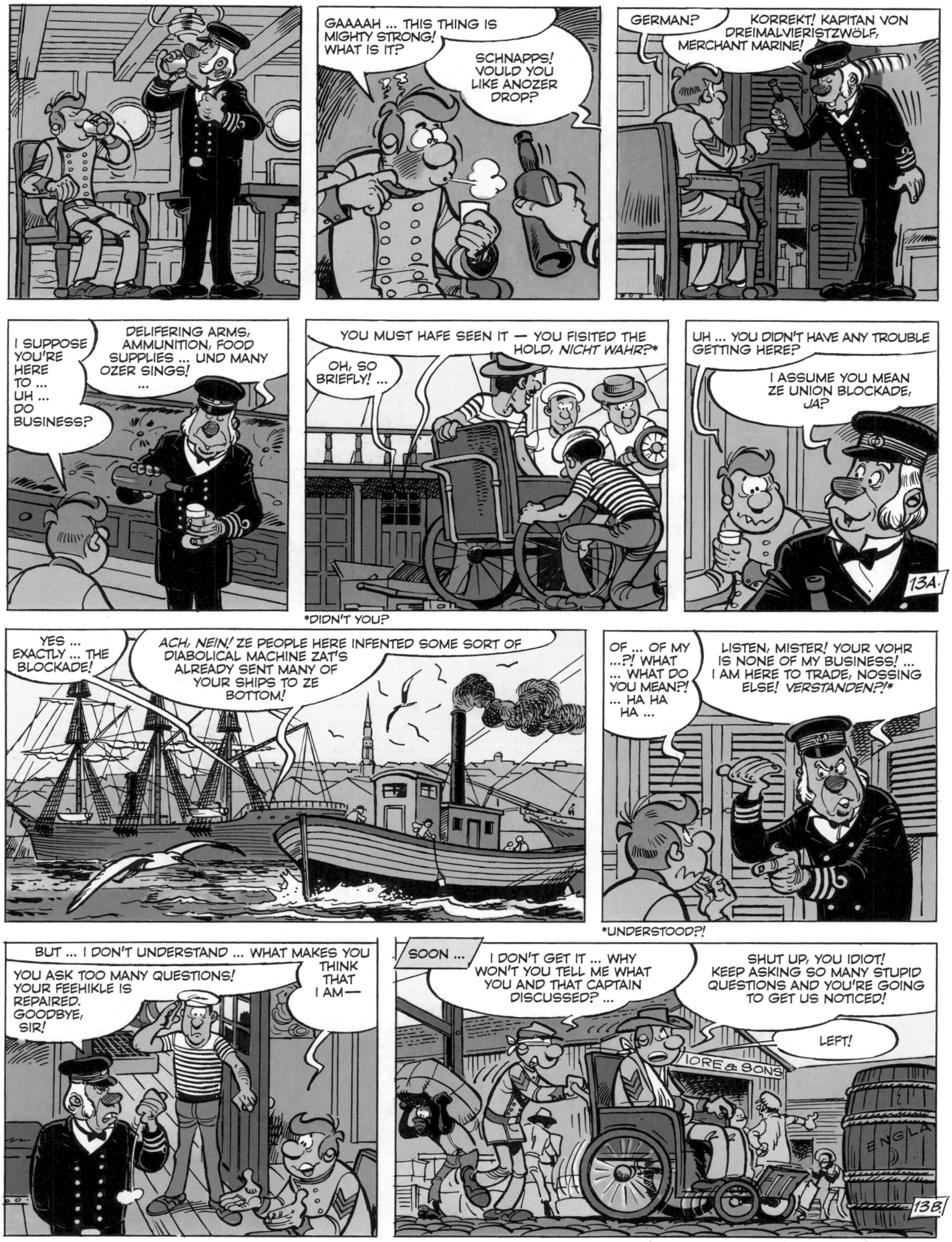
GAAAAH ... THIS THING IS MIGHTY STRONG! WHAT IS IT?
SCHNAPPS! VOULD YOU LIKE ANOZER DROP?
GERMAN?
KORREKT! KAPITAN VON DREIMALVIERISTZWÖLF, MERCHANT MARINE!
I SUPPOSE YOU'RE HERE TO ... UH ... DO BUSINESS?
DELIFERING ARMS, AMMUNITION, FOOD SUPPLIES ... UND MANY OZER SINGS! ...
YOU MUST HAFE SEEN IT — YOU FISITED THE HOLD, NICHT WAHR?*
OH, SO BRIEFLY! ...
*DIDN'T YOU?
UH ... YOU DIDN'T HAVE ANY TROUBLE GETTING HERE?
I ASSUME YOU MEAN ZE UNION BLOCKADE, JA?
13A.
YES ... EXACTLY ... THE BLOCKADE!
ACH, NEIN! ZE PEOPLE HERE INFENTED SOME SORT OF DIABOLICAL MACHINE ZAT'S ALREADY SENT MANY OF YOUR SHIPS TO ZE BOTTOM!
OF ... OF MY ...?! WHAT ... WHAT DO YOU MEAN?! ... HA HA HA ...
LISTEN, MISTER! YOUR VOHR IS NONE OF MY BUSINESS! ... I AM HERE TO TRADE, NOSSING ELSE! VERSTANDEN?!*
*UNDERSTOOD?!
BUT ... I DON'T UNDERSTAND ... WHAT MAKES YOU THINK THAT I AM—
YOU ASK TOO MANY QUESTIONS! YOUR FEEHIKLE IS REPAIRED. GOODBYE, SIR!
SOON ...
I DON'T GET IT ... WHY WON'T YOU TELL ME WHAT YOU AND THAT CAPTAIN DISCUSSED? ...
SHUT UP, YOU IDIOT! KEEP ASKING SO MANY STUPID QUESTIONS AND YOU'RE GOING TO GET US NOTICED!
LEFT!
IORE & SONS
ENGLA
13B.

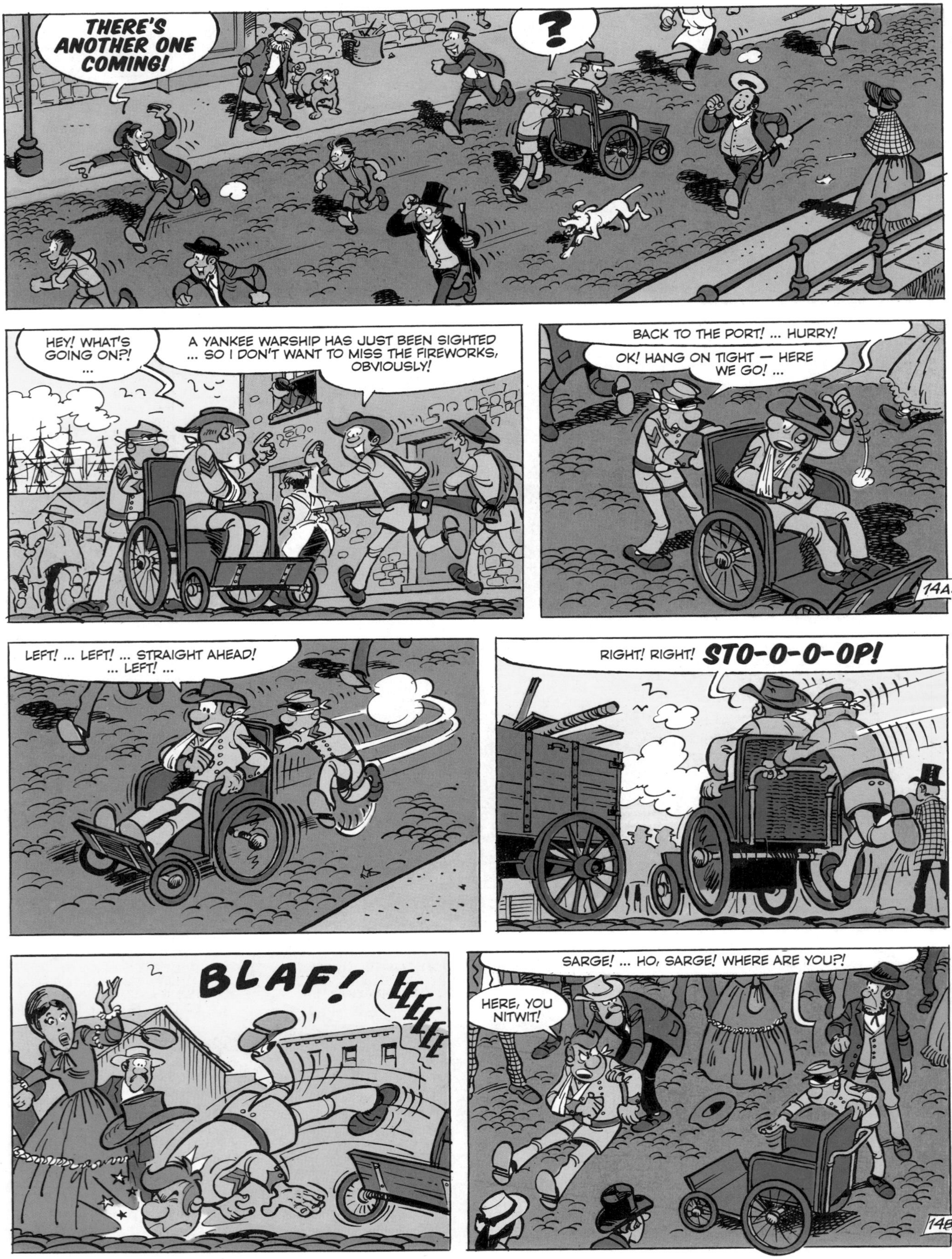
THERE'S ANOTHER ONE COMING!
?
HEY! WHAT'S GOING ON?! ...
A YANKEE WARSHIP HAS JUST BEEN SIGHTED ... SO I DON'T WANT TO MISS THE FIREWORKS, OBVIOUSLY!
BACK TO THE PORT! ... HURRY!
OK! HANG ON TIGHT — HERE WE GO! ...
14A.
LEFT! ... LEFT! ... STRAIGHT AHEAD! ... LEFT! ...
RIGHT! RIGHT! STO-O-O-OP!
BLAF!
EEEEEE
SARGE! ... HO, SARGE! WHERE ARE YOU?!
HERE, YOU NITWIT!
14B.

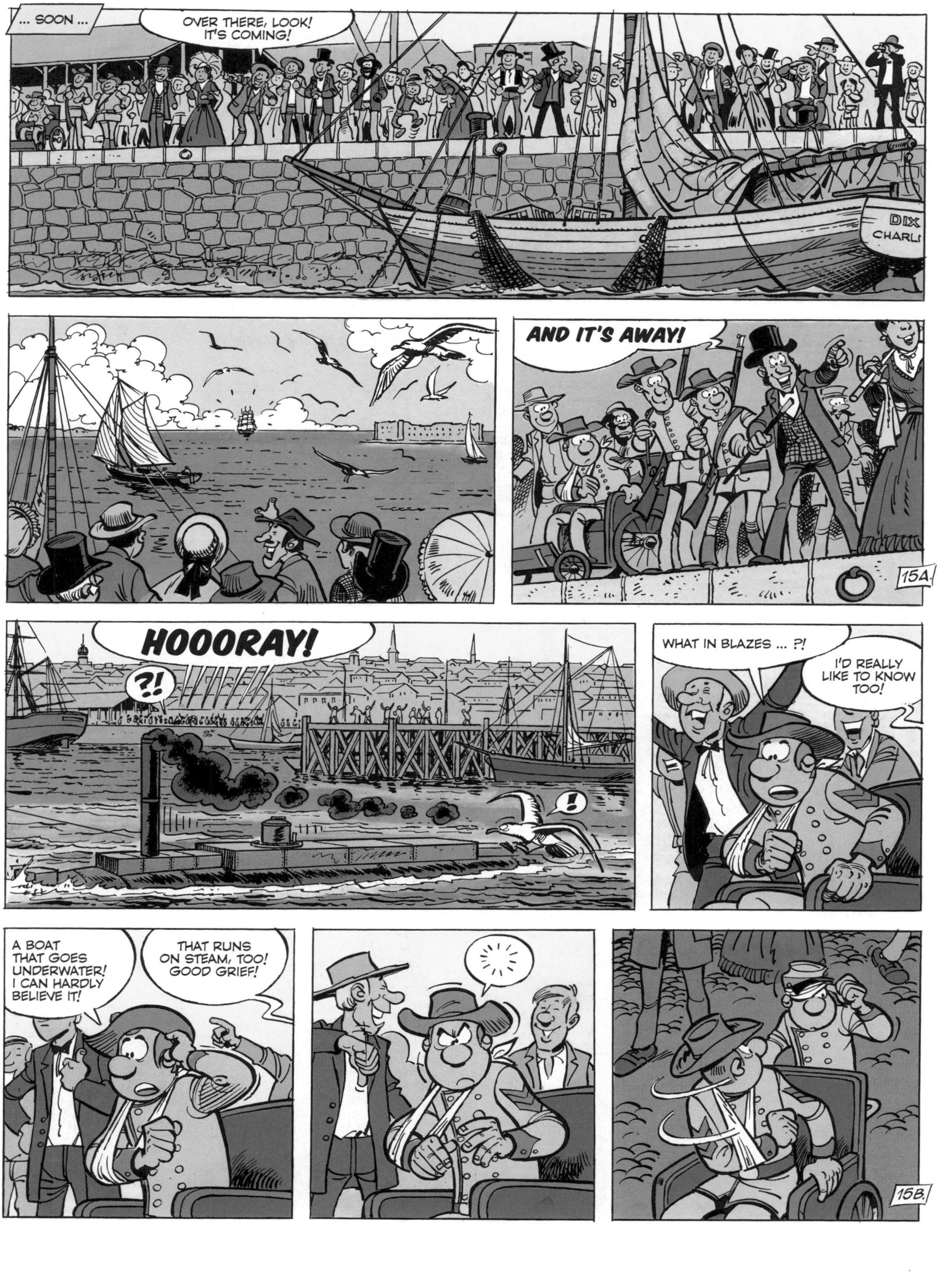
... SOON ...
OVER THERE, LOOK! IT'S COMING!
DIX
CHARLI
AND IT'S AWAY!
15A.
HOOORAY!
?!
!
WHAT IN BLAZES ... ?!
I'D REALLY LIKE TO KNOW TOO!
A BOAT THAT GOES UNDERWATER! I CAN HARDLY BELIEVE IT!
THAT RUNS ON STEAM, TOO! GOOD GRIEF!
15B.

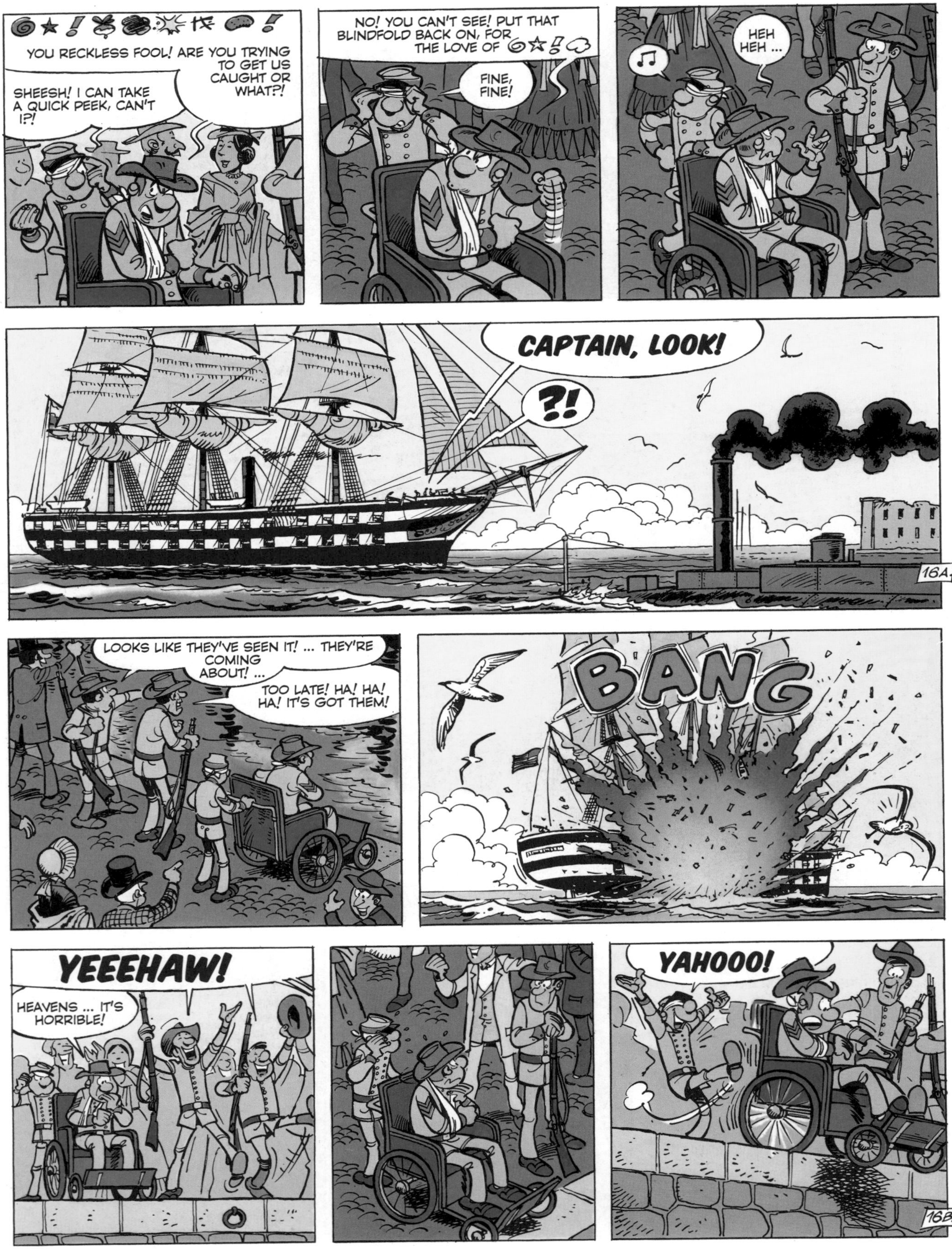
YOU RECKLESS FOOL! ARE YOU TRYING TO GET US CAUGHT OR WHAT?!
SHEESH! I CAN TAKE A QUICK PEEK, CAN'T I?!
NO! YOU CAN'T SEE! PUT THAT BLINDFOLD BACK ON, FOR THE LOVE OF
FINE, FINE!
HEH HEH ...
CAPTAIN, LOOK!
?!
16A.
LOOKS LIKE THEY'VE SEEN IT! ... THEY'RE COMING ABOUT! ...
TOO LATE! HA! HA! HA! IT'S GOT THEM!
BANG
YEEEHAW!
HEAVENS ... IT'S HORRIBLE!
YAHOOO!
16B.

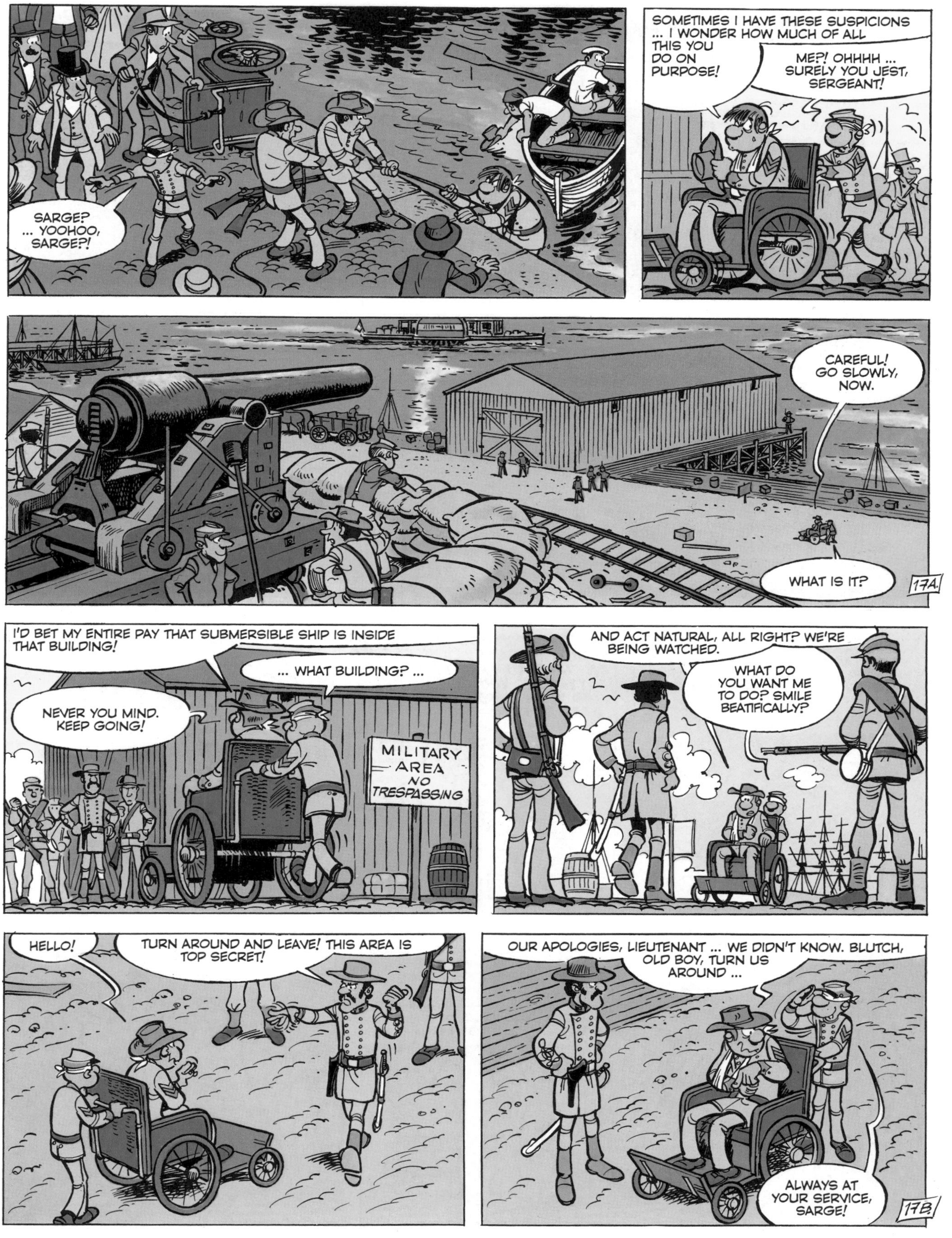
SARGE? ... YOOHOO, SARGE?!
SOMETIMES I HAVE THESE SUSPICIONS ... I WONDER HOW MUCH OF ALL THIS YOU DO ON PURPOSE!
ME?! OHHHH ... SURELY YOU JEST, SERGEANT!
CAREFUL! GO SLOWLY, NOW.
WHAT IS IT?
17A.
I'D BET MY ENTIRE PAY THAT SUBMERSIBLE SHIP IS INSIDE THAT BUILDING!
... WHAT BUILDING? ...
NEVER YOU MIND. KEEP GOING!
MILITARY AREA NO TRESPASSING
AND ACT NATURAL, ALL RIGHT? WE'RE BEING WATCHED.
WHAT DO YOU WANT ME TO DO? SMILE BEATIFICALLY?
HELLO!
TURN AROUND AND LEAVE! THIS AREA IS TOP SECRET!
OUR APOLOGIES, LIEUTENANT ... WE DIDN'T KNOW. BLUTCH, OLD BOY, TURN US AROUND ...
ALWAYS AT YOUR SERVICE, SARGE!
17B.

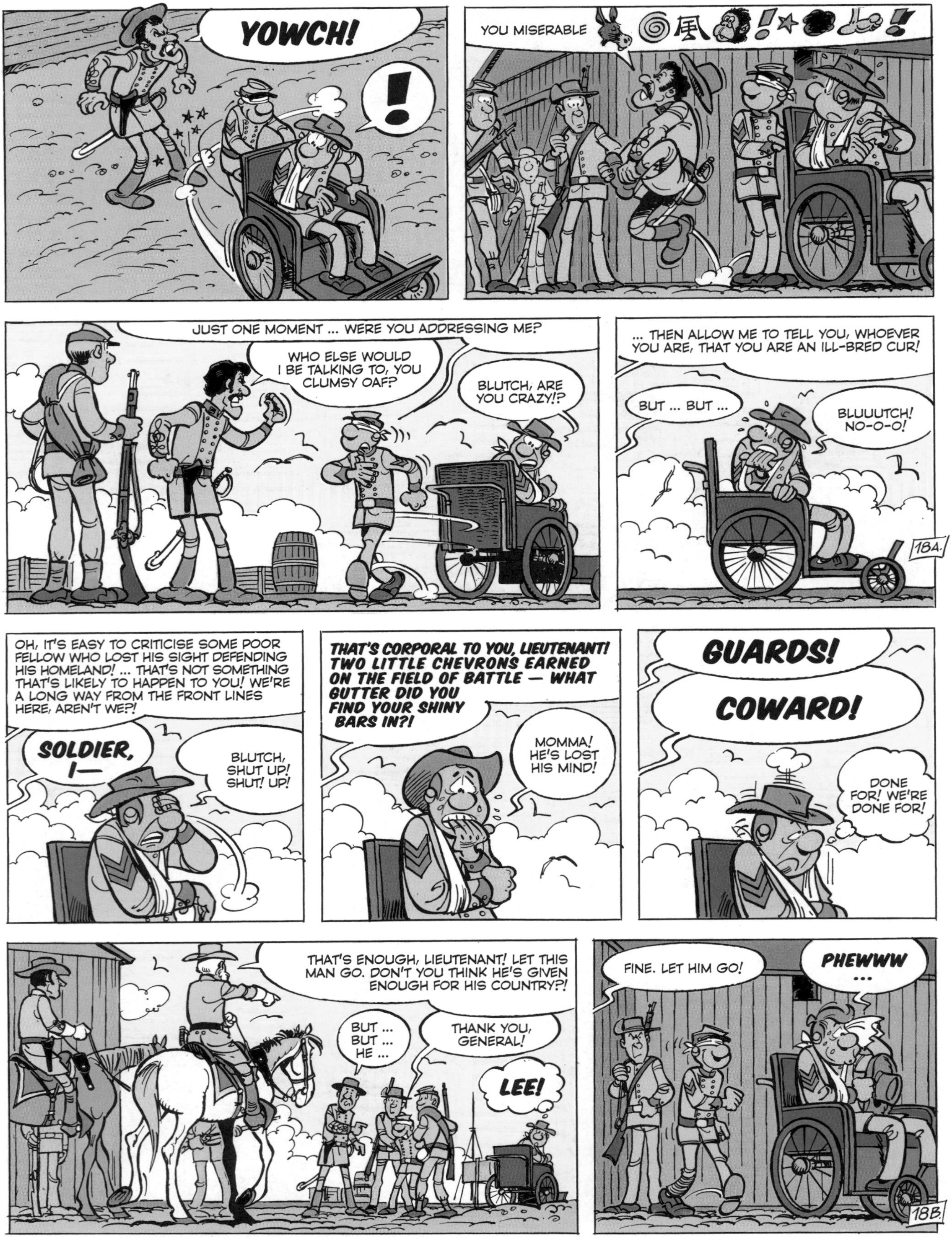
YOWCH!
!
YOU MISERABLE
JUST ONE MOMENT ... WERE YOU ADDRESSING ME?
WHO ELSE WOULD I BE TALKING TO, YOU CLUMSY OAF?
BLUTCH, ARE YOU CRAZY!?
... THEN ALLOW ME TO TELL YOU, WHOEVER YOU ARE, THAT YOU ARE AN ILL-BRED CUR!
BUT ... BUT ...
BLUUUTCH! NO-O-O!
18A.
OH, IT'S EASY TO CRITICISE SOME POOR FELLOW WHO LOST HIS SIGHT DEFENDING HIS HOMELAND! ... THAT'S NOT SOMETHING THAT'S LIKELY TO HAPPEN TO YOU! WE'RE A LONG WAY FROM THE FRONT LINES HERE, AREN'T WE?!
SOLDIER, I—
BLUTCH, SHUT UP! SHUT! UP!
THAT'S CORPORAL TO YOU, LIEUTENANT! TWO LITTLE CHEVRONS EARNED ON THE FIELD OF BATTLE — WHAT GUTTER DID YOU FIND YOUR SHINY BARS IN?!
MOMMA! HE'S LOST HIS MIND!
GUARDS!
COWARD!
DONE FOR! WE'RE DONE FOR!
THAT'S ENOUGH, LIEUTENANT! LET THIS MAN GO. DON'T YOU THINK HE'S GIVEN ENOUGH FOR HIS COUNTRY?!
BUT ... BUT ... HE ...
THANK YOU, GENERAL!
LEE!
FINE. LET HIM GO!
PHEWWW ...
18B.

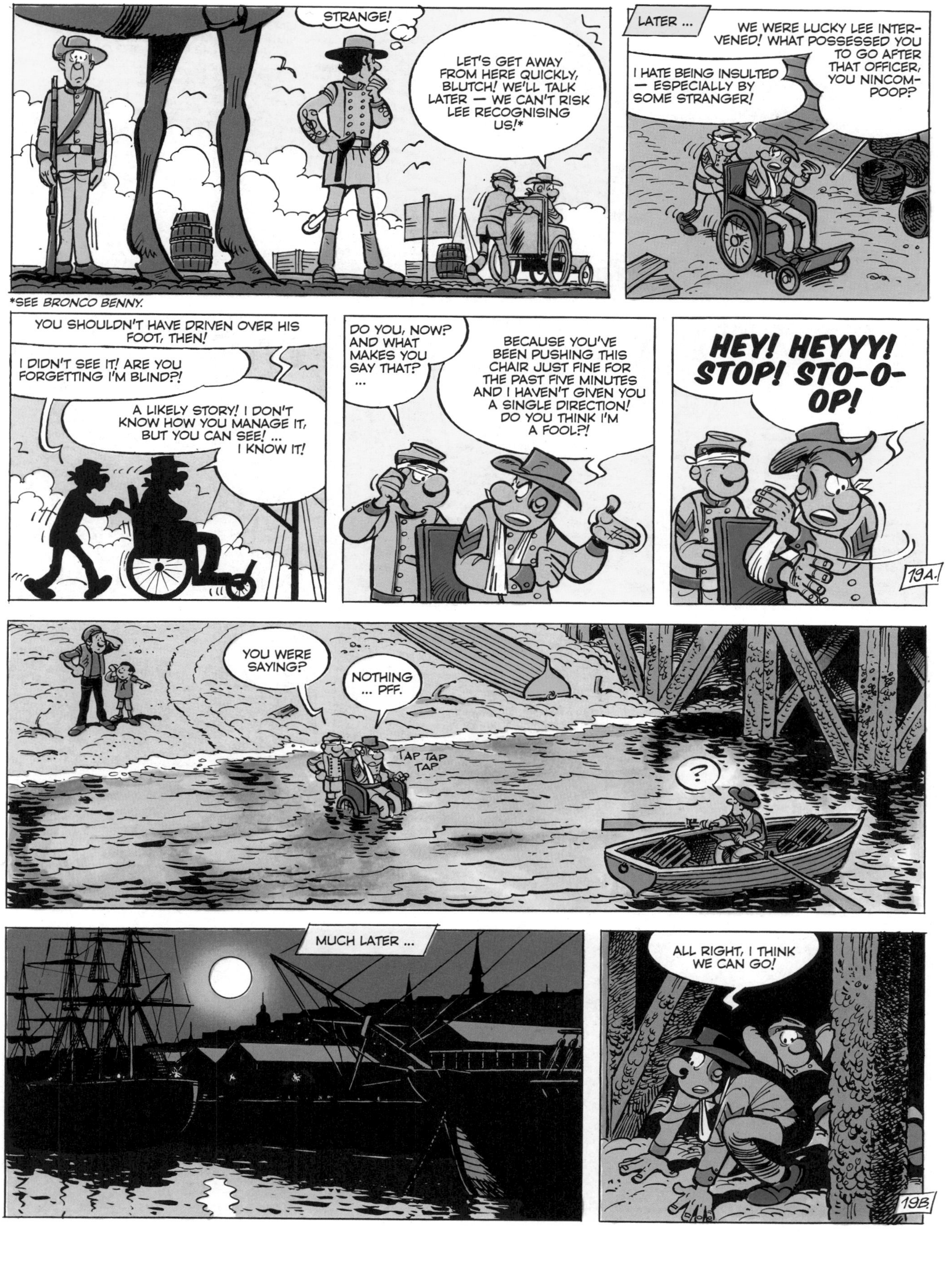
STRANGE!
LET'S GET AWAY FROM HERE QUICKLY, BLUTCH! WE'LL TALK LATER — WE CAN'T RISK LEE RECOGNISING US!*
LATER ...
WE WERE LUCKY LEE INTERVENED! WHAT POSSESSED YOU TO GO AFTER THAT OFFICER, YOU NINCOMPOOP?
I HATE BEING INSULTED — ESPECIALLY BY SOME STRANGER!
*SEE BRONCO BENNY.
YOU SHOULDN'T HAVE DRIVEN OVER HIS FOOT, THEN!
I DIDN'T SEE IT! ARE YOU FORGETTING I'M BLIND?!
A LIKELY STORY! I DON'T KNOW HOW YOU MANAGE IT, BUT YOU CAN SEE! ... I KNOW IT!
DO YOU, NOW? AND WHAT MAKES YOU SAY THAT? ...
BECAUSE YOU'VE BEEN PUSHING THIS CHAIR JUST FINE FOR THE PAST FIVE MINUTES AND I HAVEN'T GIVEN YOU A SINGLE DIRECTION! DO YOU THINK I'M A FOOL?!
HEY! HEYYY! STOP! STO-O-OP!
19A.
YOU WERE SAYING?
NOTHING ... PFF.
TAP TAP TAP
?
MUCH LATER ...
ALL RIGHT, I THINK WE CAN GO!
19B.

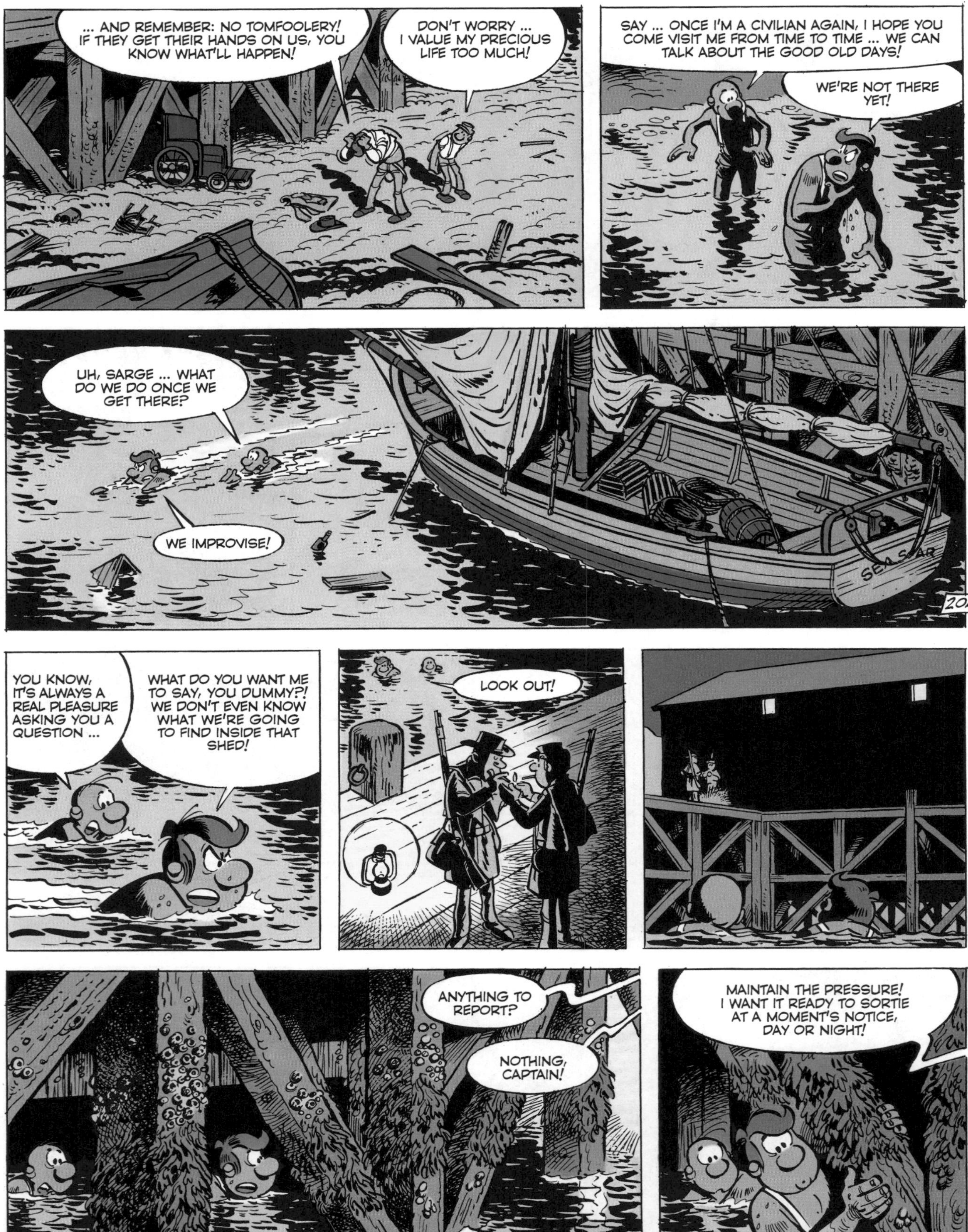
... AND REMEMBER: NO TOMFOOLERY! IF THEY GET THEIR HANDS ON US, YOU KNOW WHAT'LL HAPPEN!
DON'T WORRY ... I VALUE MY PRECIOUS LIFE TOO MUCH!
SAY ... ONCE I'M A CIVILIAN AGAIN, I HOPE YOU COME VISIT ME FROM TIME TO TIME ... WE CAN TALK ABOUT THE GOOD OLD DAYS!
WE'RE NOT THERE YET!
UH, SARGE ... WHAT DO WE DO ONCE WE GET THERE?
WE IMPROVISE!
20A
YOU KNOW, IT'S ALWAYS A REAL PLEASURE ASKING YOU A QUESTION ...
WHAT DO YOU WANT ME TO SAY, YOU DUMMY?! WE DON'T EVEN KNOW WHAT WE'RE GOING TO FIND INSIDE THAT SHED!
LOOK OUT!
ANYTHING TO REPORT?
NOTHING, CAPTAIN!
MAINTAIN THE PRESSURE! I WANT IT READY TO SORTIE AT A MOMENT'S NOTICE, DAY OR NIGHT!
20B.

SO, THIS IS THE FAMOUS *DAVID* ... ?

THAT'S RIGHT, GENERAL. IT'S STEAM-POWERED AND CARRIES ENOUGH COAL FOR ABOUT THREE HOURS. IT HAS A CREW OF FIVE OR SIX MEN.

21A.

SO, TELL ME ... HOW DO YOU GO ABOUT SINKING ENEMY SHIPS, EXACTLY?

ONCE ONE HAS BEEN SIGHTED, THE SUB-MERSIBLE IS PUT INTO THE WATER ...

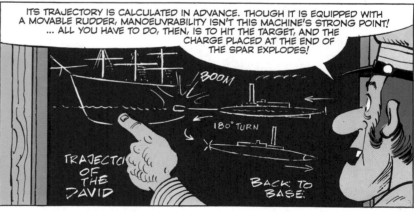

ITS TRAJECTORY IS CALCULATED IN ADVANCE. THOUGH IT IS EQUIPPED WITH A MOVABLE RUDDER, MANOEUVRABILITY ISN'T THIS MACHINE'S STRONG POINT! ... ALL YOU HAVE TO DO, THEN, IS TO HIT THE TARGET, AND THE CHARGE PLACED AT THE END OF THE SPAR EXPLODES!

BOOM

180° TURN

TRAJECTORY OF THE *DAVID*

BACK TO BASE.

IT'S DIABOLICALLY SIMPLE!

YET EXTREMELY EFFECTIVE! ASK THE YANKEES — THEY KNOW!

UNBELIEVABLE! YOU'VE GOT TO BE SICK IN THE HEAD TO INVENT SOMETHING LIKE THAT!

WHAT CAN I SAY, BLUTCH? ... SOME PEOPLE WERE BORN SADISTIC AND WILL DIE SADISTIC!

21B.

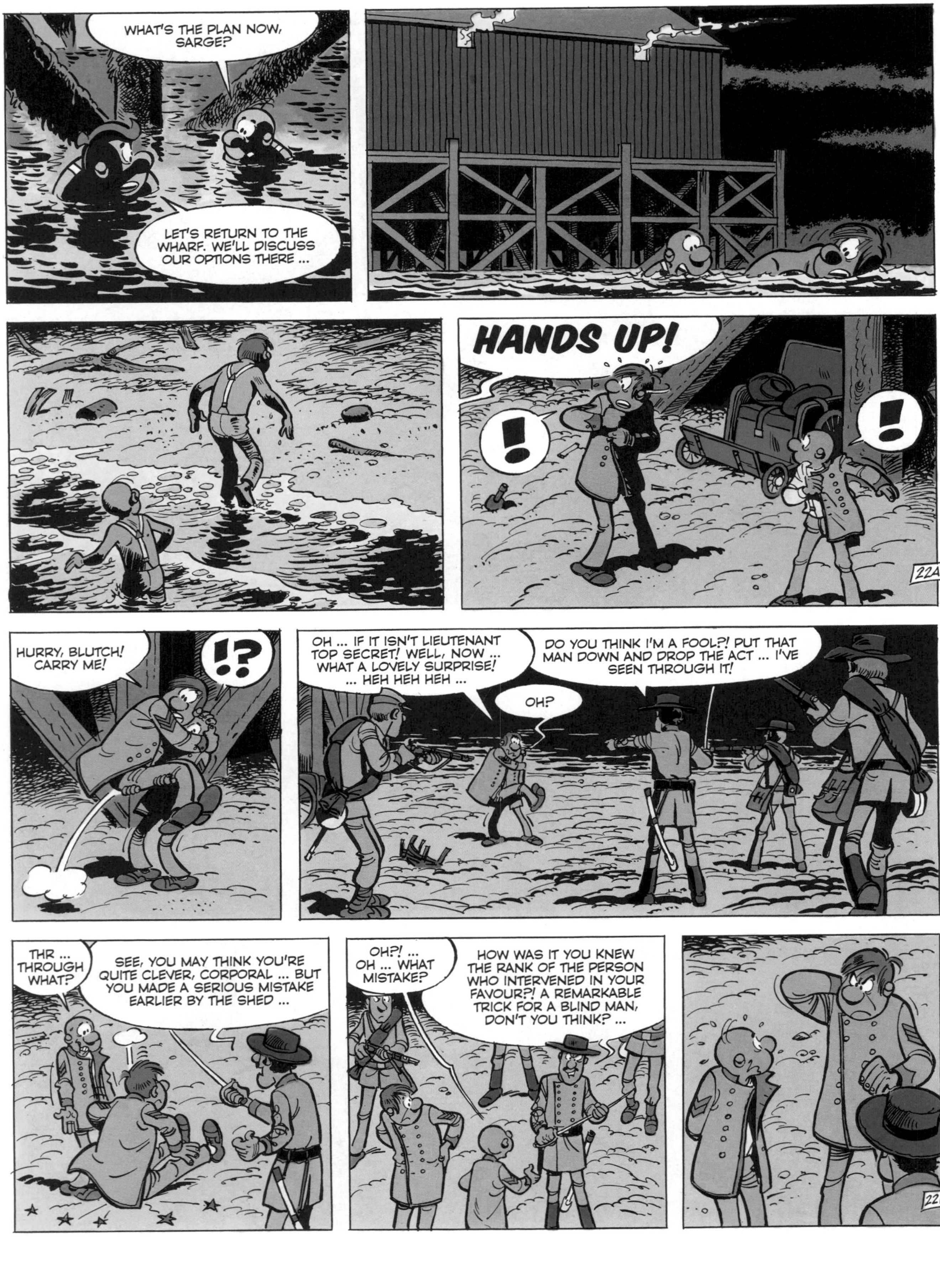

WHAT'S THE PLAN NOW, SARGE?
LET'S RETURN TO THE WHARF. WE'LL DISCUSS OUR OPTIONS THERE ...
HANDS UP!
!
!
22A.
HURRY, BLUTCH! CARRY ME!
!?
OH ... IF IT ISN'T LIEUTENANT TOP SECRET! WELL, NOW ... WHAT A LOVELY SURPRISE! ... HEH HEH HEH ...
OH?
DO YOU THINK I'M A FOOL?! PUT THAT MAN DOWN AND DROP THE ACT ... I'VE SEEN THROUGH IT!
THR ... THROUGH WHAT?
SEE, YOU MAY THINK YOU'RE QUITE CLEVER, CORPORAL ... BUT YOU MADE A SERIOUS MISTAKE EARLIER BY THE SHED ...
OH?! ... OH ... WHAT MISTAKE?
HOW WAS IT YOU KNEW THE RANK OF THE PERSON WHO INTERVENED IN YOUR FAVOUR?! A REMARKABLE TRICK FOR A BLIND MAN, DON'T YOU THINK? ...
22B.

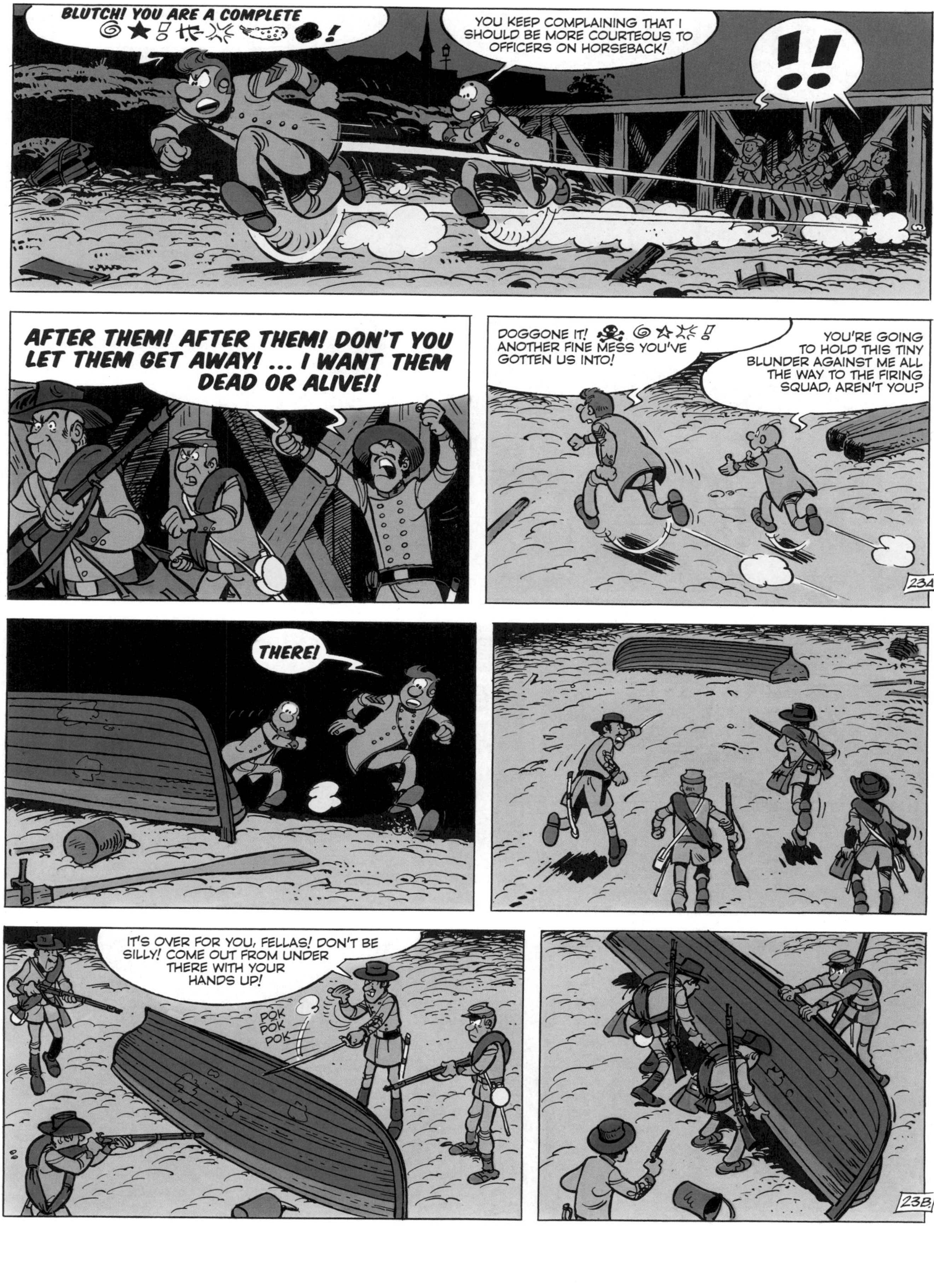
BLUTCH! YOU ARE A COMPLETE ★!!
YOU KEEP COMPLAINING THAT I SHOULD BE MORE COURTEOUS TO OFFICERS ON HORSEBACK!
!!
AFTER THEM! AFTER THEM! DON'T YOU LET THEM GET AWAY! ... I WANT THEM DEAD OR ALIVE!!
DOGGONE IT! ☆! ANOTHER FINE MESS YOU'VE GOTTEN US INTO!
YOU'RE GOING TO HOLD THIS TINY BLUNDER AGAINST ME ALL THE WAY TO THE FIRING SQUAD, AREN'T YOU?
23A.
THERE!
IT'S OVER FOR YOU, FELLAS! DON'T BE SILLY! COME OUT FROM UNDER THERE WITH YOUR HANDS UP!
POK POK POK
23B.

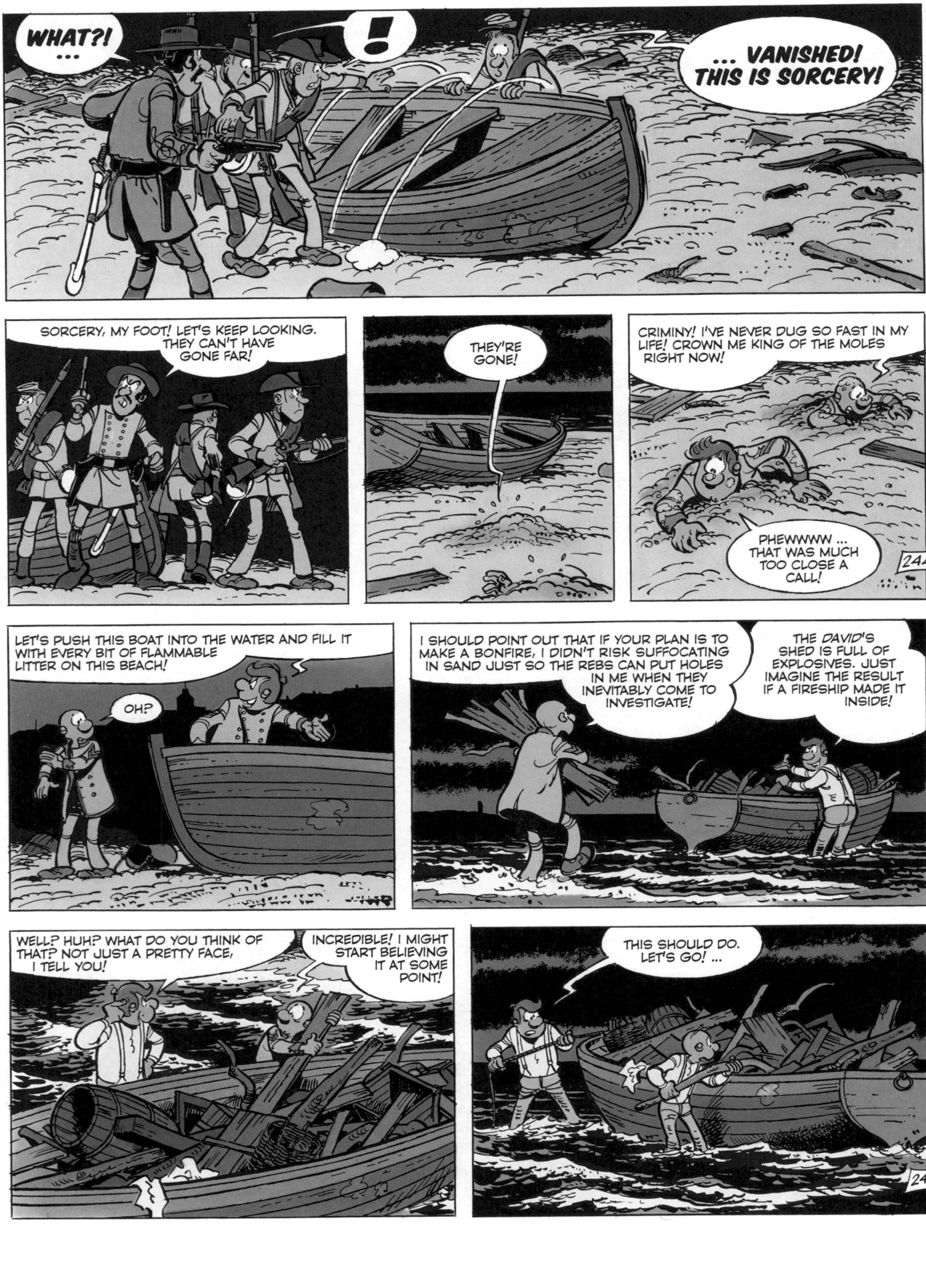
WHAT?! ...
!
... VANISHED! THIS IS SORCERY!
SORCERY, MY FOOT! LET'S KEEP LOOKING. THEY CAN'T HAVE GONE FAR!
THEY'RE GONE!
CRIMINY! I'VE NEVER DUG SO FAST IN MY LIFE! CROWN ME KING OF THE MOLES RIGHT NOW!
PHEWWWW ... THAT WAS MUCH TOO CLOSE A CALL!
24A.
LET'S PUSH THIS BOAT INTO THE WATER AND FILL IT WITH EVERY BIT OF FLAMMABLE LITTER ON THIS BEACH!
OH?
I SHOULD POINT OUT THAT IF YOUR PLAN IS TO MAKE A BONFIRE, I DIDN'T RISK SUFFOCATING IN SAND JUST SO THE REBS CAN PUT HOLES IN ME WHEN THEY INEVITABLY COME TO INVESTIGATE!
THE *DAVID*'S SHED IS FULL OF EXPLOSIVES. JUST IMAGINE THE RESULT IF A FIRESHIP MADE IT INSIDE!
WELL? HUH? WHAT DO YOU THINK OF THAT? NOT JUST A PRETTY FACE, I TELL YOU!
INCREDIBLE! I MIGHT START BELIEVING IT AT SOME POINT!
THIS SHOULD DO. LET'S GO! ...
24B.

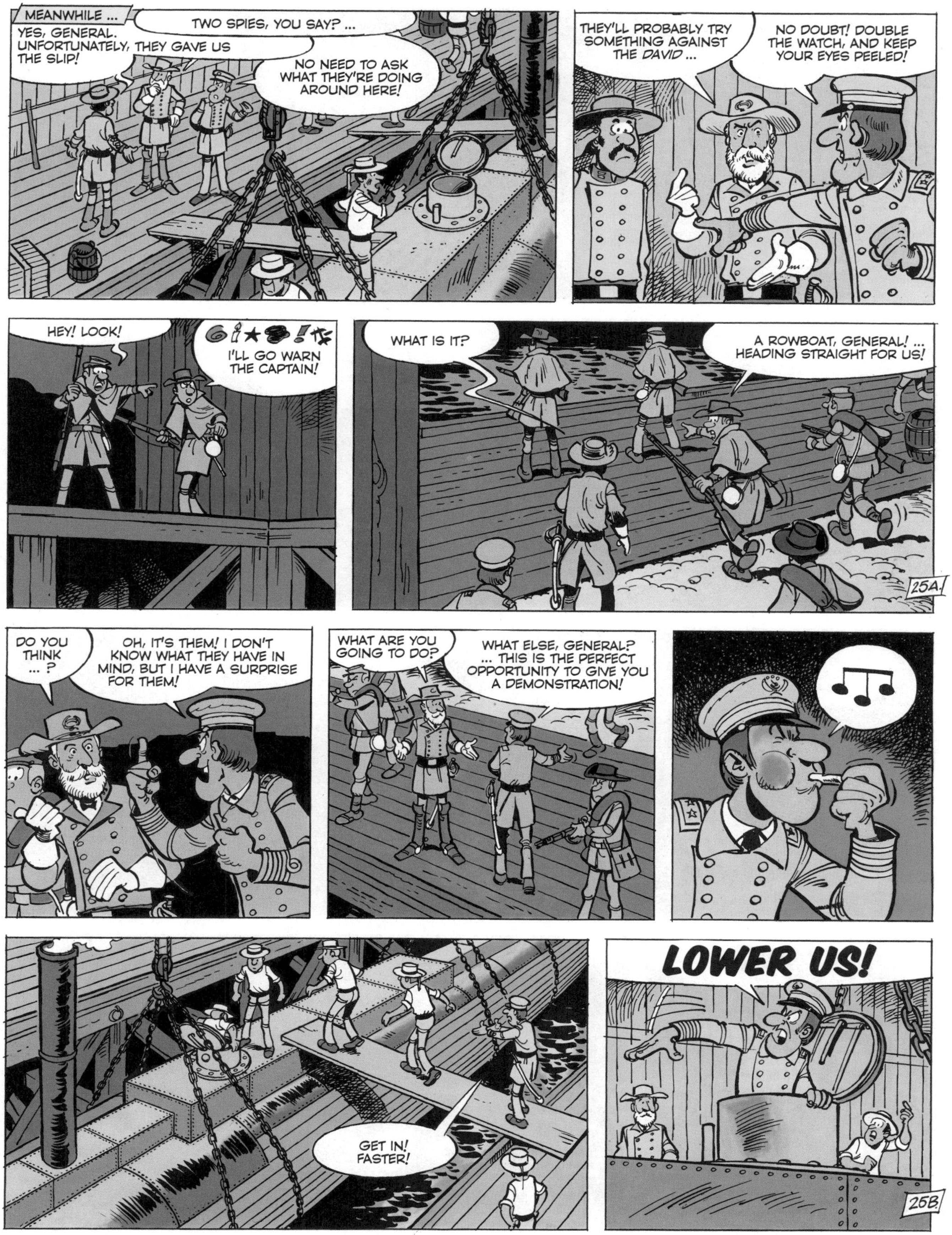
MEANWHILE ...
TWO SPIES, YOU SAY? ...
YES, GENERAL. UNFORTUNATELY, THEY GAVE US THE SLIP!
NO NEED TO ASK WHAT THEY'RE DOING AROUND HERE!
THEY'LL PROBABLY TRY SOMETHING AGAINST THE *DAVID* ...
NO DOUBT! DOUBLE THE WATCH, AND KEEP YOUR EYES PEELED!
HEY! LOOK!
I'LL GO WARN THE CAPTAIN!
WHAT IS IT?
A ROWBOAT, GENERAL! ... HEADING STRAIGHT FOR US!
25A.
DO YOU THINK ... ?
OH, IT'S THEM! I DON'T KNOW WHAT THEY HAVE IN MIND, BUT I HAVE A SURPRISE FOR THEM!
WHAT ARE YOU GOING TO DO?
WHAT ELSE, GENERAL? ... THIS IS THE PERFECT OPPORTUNITY TO GIVE YOU A DEMONSTRATION!
GET IN! FASTER!
LOWER US!
25B.

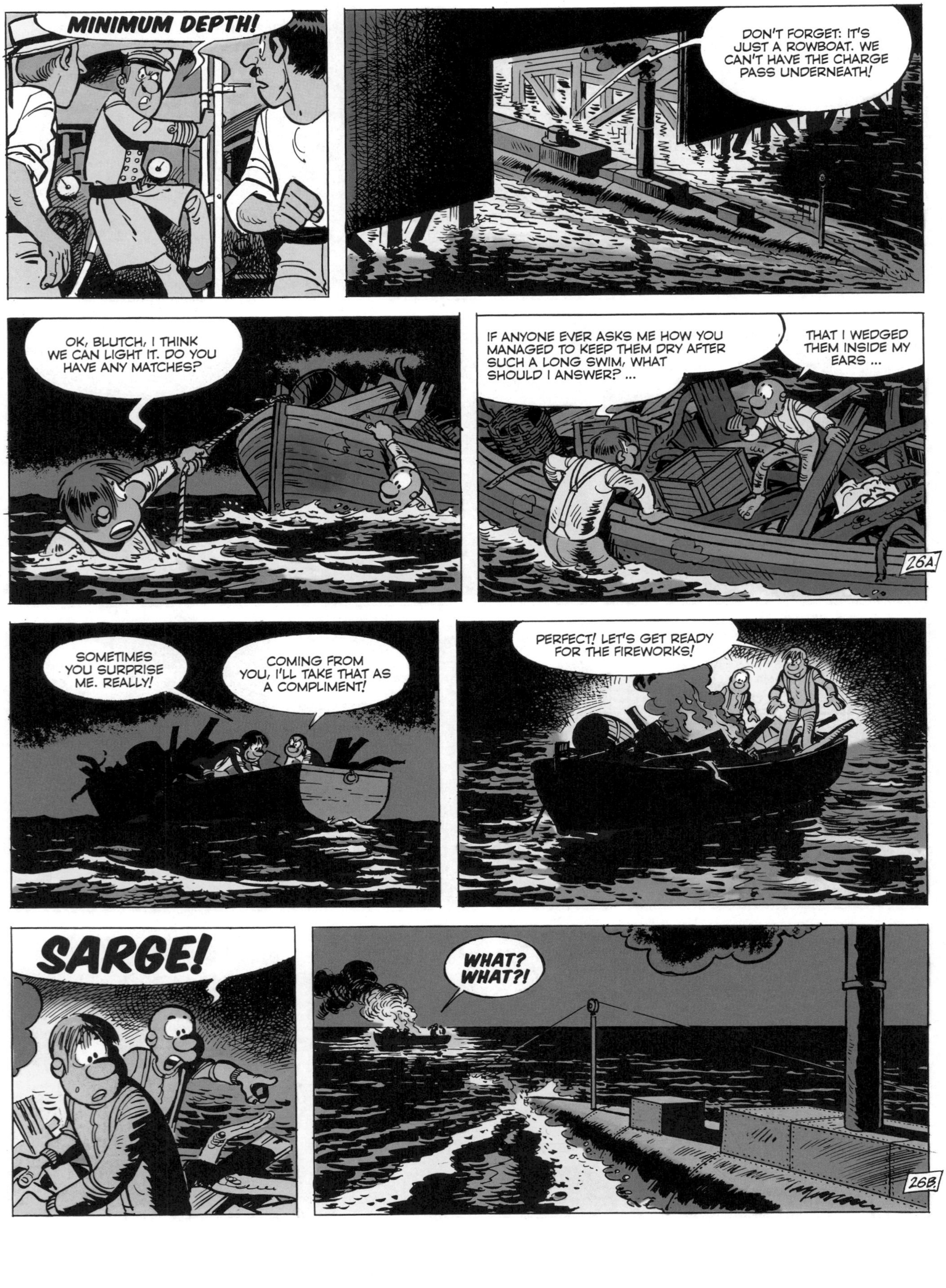
MINIMUM DEPTH!
DON'T FORGET: IT'S JUST A ROWBOAT. WE CAN'T HAVE THE CHARGE PASS UNDERNEATH!
OK, BLUTCH, I THINK WE CAN LIGHT IT. DO YOU HAVE ANY MATCHES?
IF ANYONE EVER ASKS ME HOW YOU MANAGED TO KEEP THEM DRY AFTER SUCH A LONG SWIM, WHAT SHOULD I ANSWER? ...
THAT I WEDGED THEM INSIDE MY EARS ...
26A.
SOMETIMES YOU SURPRISE ME. REALLY!
COMING FROM YOU, I'LL TAKE THAT AS A COMPLIMENT!
PERFECT! LET'S GET READY FOR THE FIREWORKS!
SARGE!
WHAT? WHAT?!
26B.

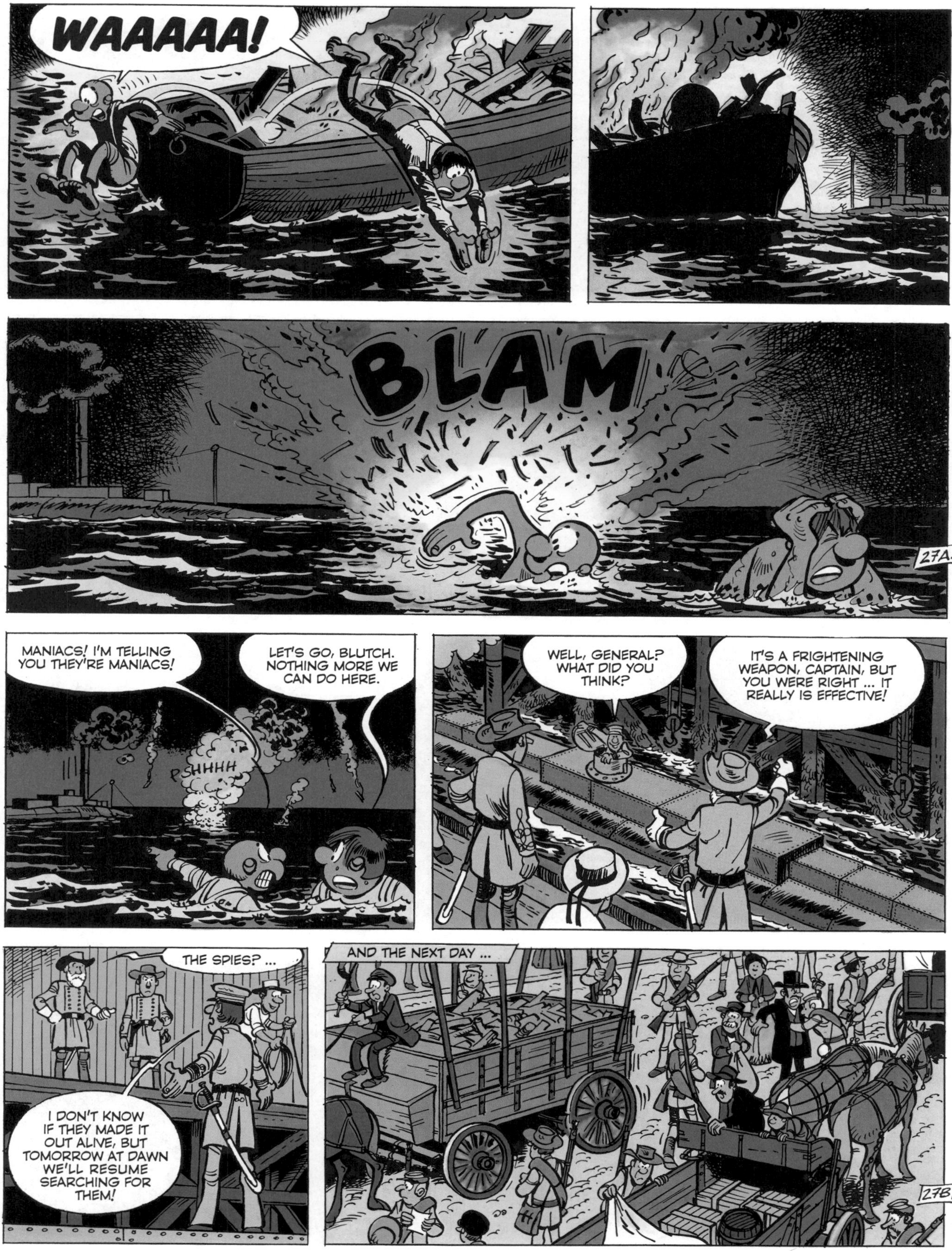
WAAAAA!
BLAM
27A.
MANIACS! I'M TELLING YOU THEY'RE MANIACS!
LET'S GO, BLUTCH. NOTHING MORE WE CAN DO HERE.
PSHHHH
WELL, GENERAL? WHAT DID YOU THINK?
IT'S A FRIGHTENING WEAPON, CAPTAIN, BUT YOU WERE RIGHT ... IT REALLY IS EFFECTIVE!
THE SPIES? ...
I DON'T KNOW IF THEY MADE IT OUT ALIVE, BUT TOMORROW AT DAWN WE'LL RESUME SEARCHING FOR THEM!
AND THE NEXT DAY ...
27B

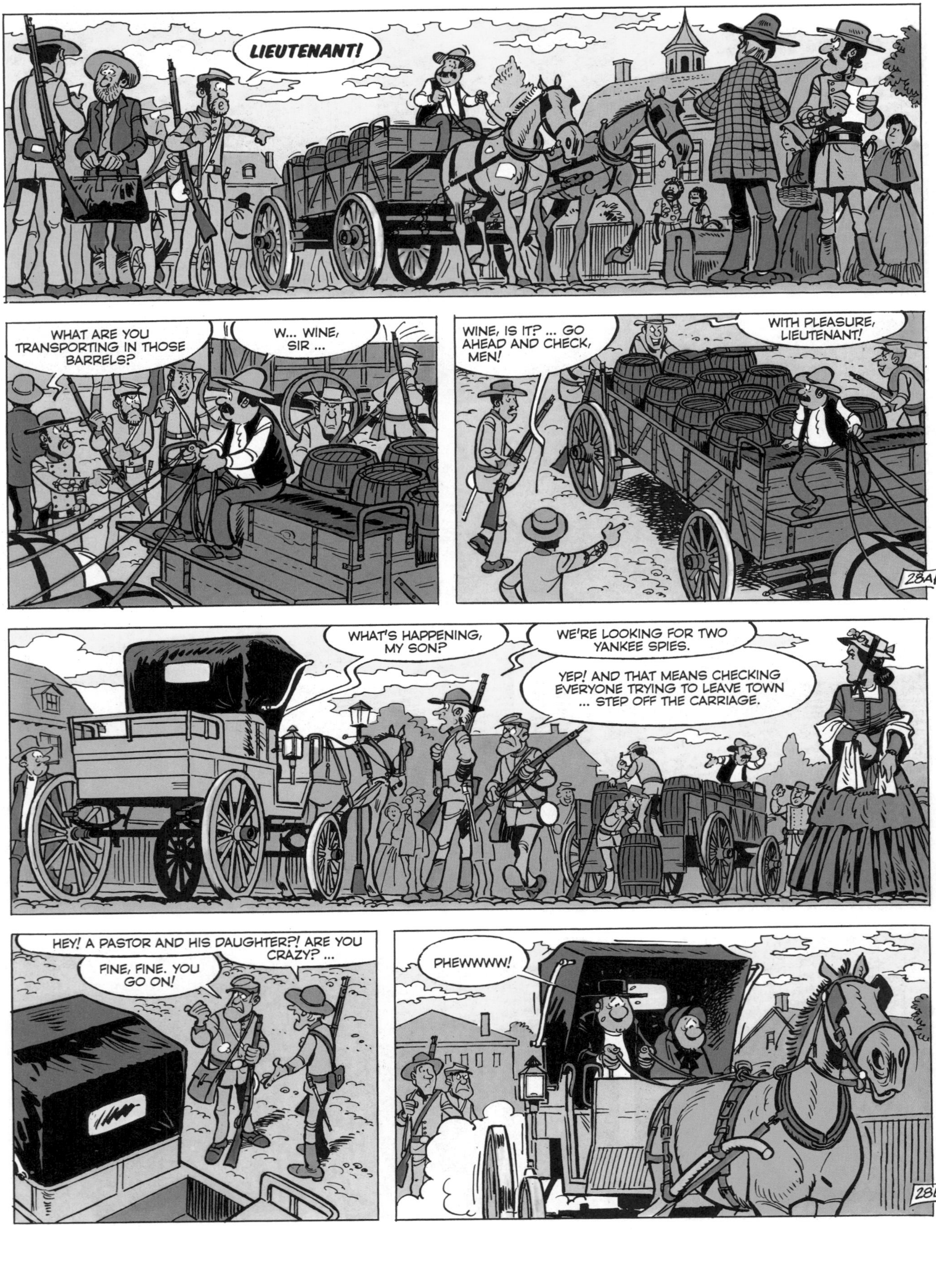
LIEUTENANT!
WHAT ARE YOU TRANSPORTING IN THOSE BARRELS?
W... WINE, SIR ...
WINE, IS IT? ... GO AHEAD AND CHECK, MEN!
WITH PLEASURE, LIEUTENANT!
28A
WHAT'S HAPPENING, MY SON?
WE'RE LOOKING FOR TWO YANKEE SPIES.
YEP! AND THAT MEANS CHECKING EVERYONE TRYING TO LEAVE TOWN ... STEP OFF THE CARRIAGE.
HEY! A PASTOR AND HIS DAUGHTER?! ARE YOU CRAZY? ...
FINE, FINE. YOU GO ON!
PHEWWWW!
28B

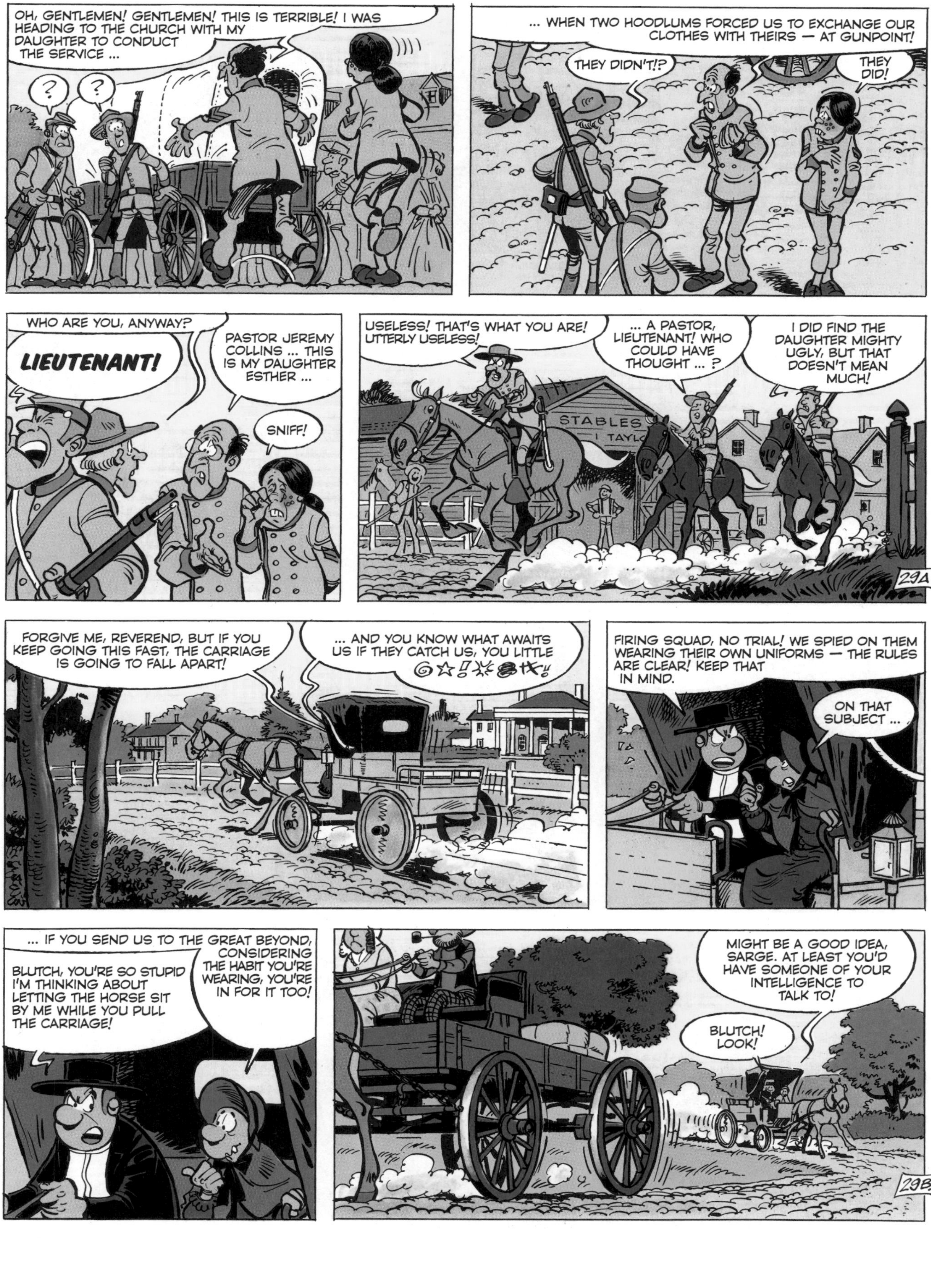
OH, GENTLEMEN! GENTLEMEN! THIS IS TERRIBLE! I WAS HEADING TO THE CHURCH WITH MY DAUGHTER TO CONDUCT THE SERVICE ...
?
?
... WHEN TWO HOODLUMS FORCED US TO EXCHANGE OUR CLOTHES WITH THEIRS — AT GUNPOINT!
THEY DIDN'T!?
THEY DID!
WHO ARE YOU, ANYWAY?
LIEUTENANT!
PASTOR JEREMY COLLINS ... THIS IS MY DAUGHTER ESTHER ...
SNIFF!
USELESS! THAT'S WHAT YOU ARE! UTTERLY USELESS!
... A PASTOR, LIEUTENANT! WHO COULD HAVE THOUGHT ... ?
I DID FIND THE DAUGHTER MIGHTY UGLY, BUT THAT DOESN'T MEAN MUCH!
STABLES
29A!
FORGIVE ME, REVEREND, BUT IF YOU KEEP GOING THIS FAST, THE CARRIAGE IS GOING TO FALL APART!
... AND YOU KNOW WHAT AWAITS US IF THEY CATCH US, YOU LITTLE
FIRING SQUAD, NO TRIAL! WE SPIED ON THEM WEARING THEIR OWN UNIFORMS — THE RULES ARE CLEAR! KEEP THAT IN MIND.
ON THAT SUBJECT ...
... IF YOU SEND US TO THE GREAT BEYOND, CONSIDERING THE HABIT YOU'RE WEARING, YOU'RE IN FOR IT TOO!
BLUTCH, YOU'RE SO STUPID I'M THINKING ABOUT LETTING THE HORSE SIT BY ME WHILE YOU PULL THE CARRIAGE!
MIGHT BE A GOOD IDEA, SARGE. AT LEAST YOU'D HAVE SOMEONE OF YOUR INTELLIGENCE TO TALK TO!
BLUTCH! LOOK!
29B!

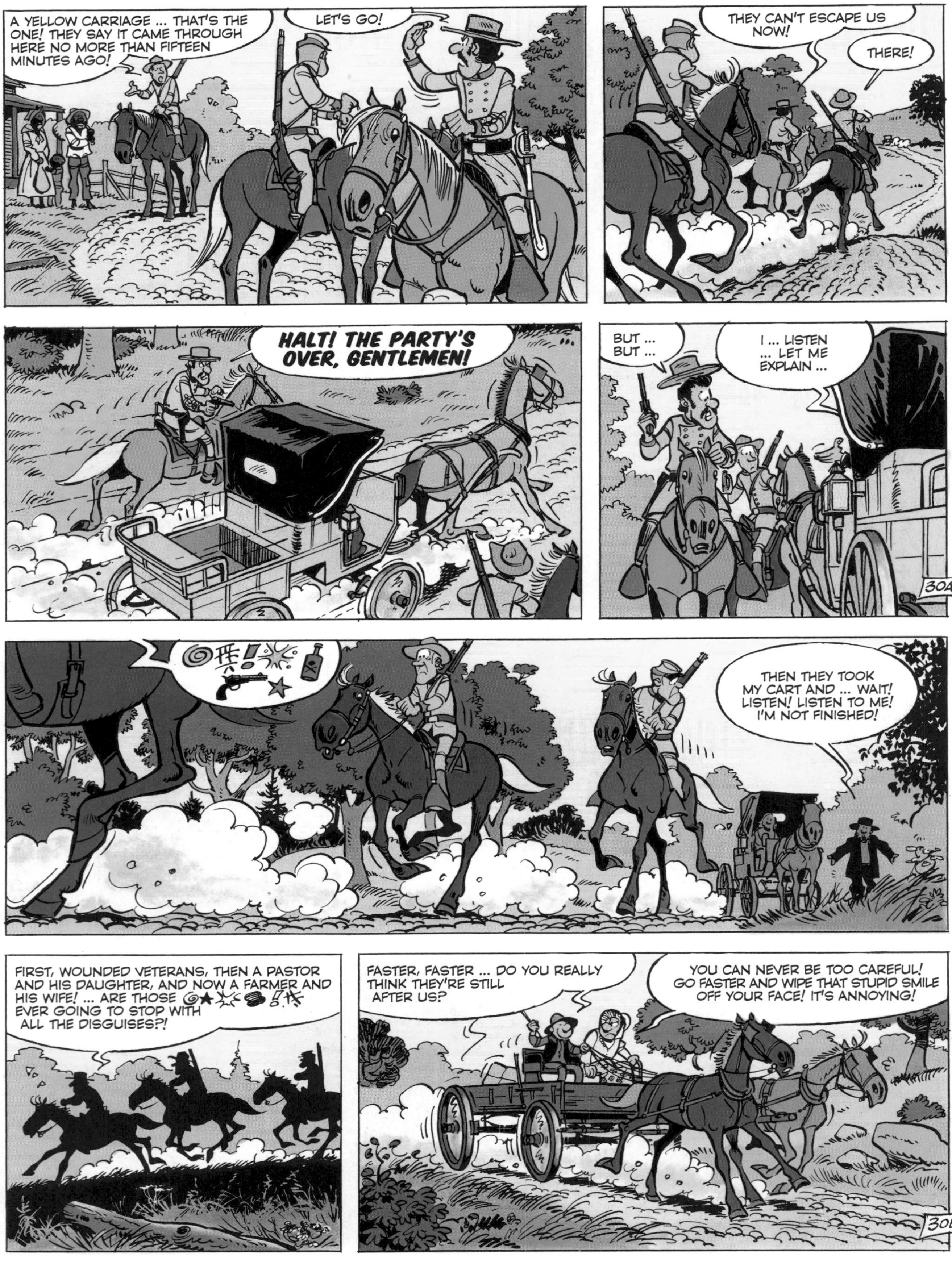
A YELLOW CARRIAGE ... THAT'S THE ONE! THEY SAY IT CAME THROUGH HERE NO MORE THAN FIFTEEN MINUTES AGO!
LET'S GO!
THEY CAN'T ESCAPE US NOW!
THERE!
HALT! THE PARTY'S OVER, GENTLEMEN!
BUT ... BUT ...
I ... LISTEN ... LET ME EXPLAIN ...
30A
THEN THEY TOOK MY CART AND ... WAIT! LISTEN! LISTEN TO ME! I'M NOT FINISHED!
FIRST, WOUNDED VETERANS, THEN A PASTOR AND HIS DAUGHTER, AND NOW A FARMER AND HIS WIFE! ... ARE THOSE EVER GOING TO STOP WITH ALL THE DISGUISES?!
FASTER, FASTER ... DO YOU REALLY THINK THEY'RE STILL AFTER US?
YOU CAN NEVER BE TOO CAREFUL! GO FASTER AND WIPE THAT STUPID SMILE OFF YOUR FACE! IT'S ANNOYING!
30B

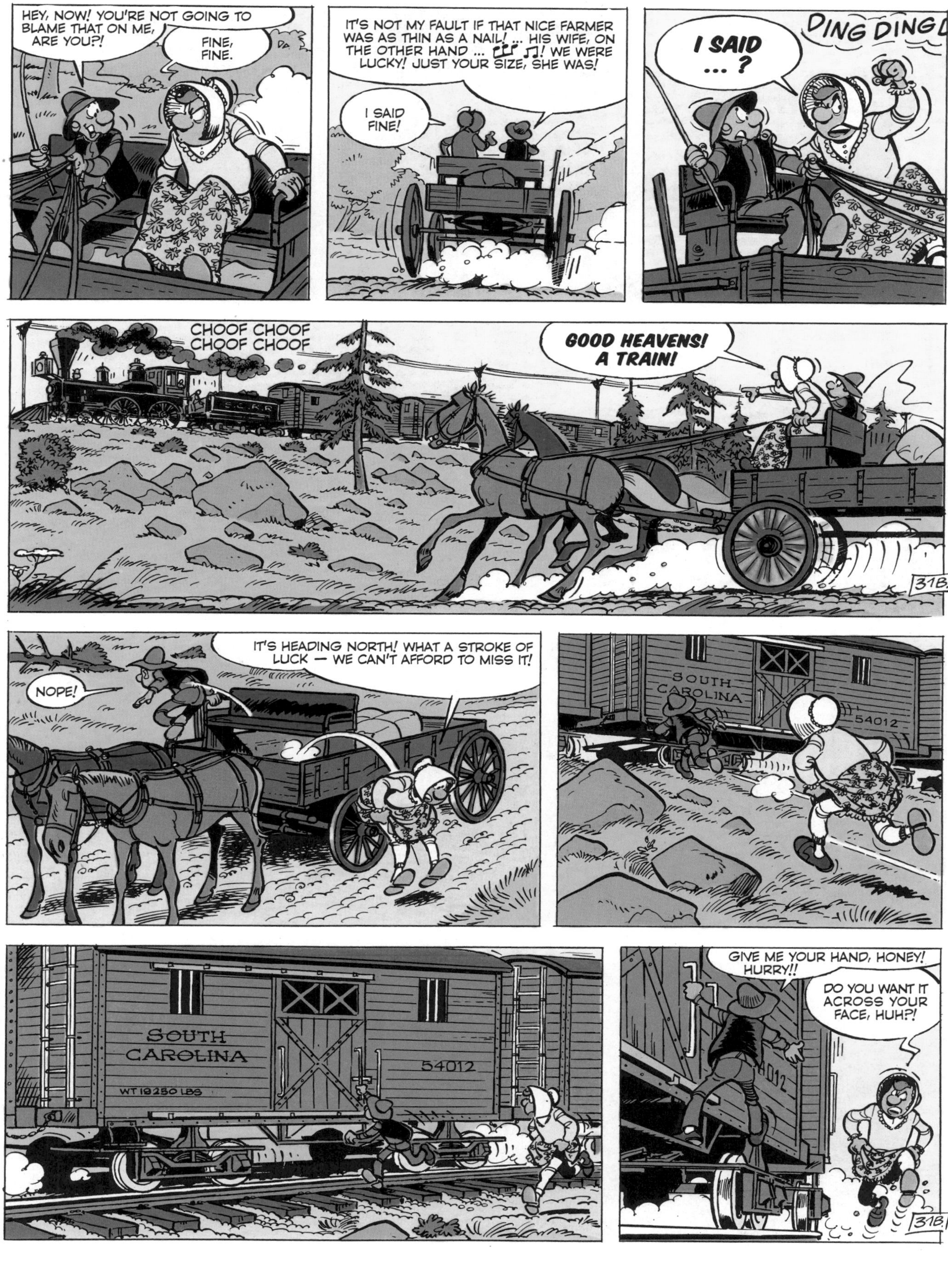
HEY, NOW! YOU'RE NOT GOING TO BLAME THAT ON ME, ARE YOU?!
FINE, FINE.
IT'S NOT MY FAULT IF THAT NICE FARMER WAS AS THIN AS A NAIL! ... HIS WIFE, ON THE OTHER HAND ... ♫♫! WE WERE LUCKY! JUST YOUR SIZE, SHE WAS!
I SAID FINE!
I SAID ... ?
DING DING
CHOOF CHOOF CHOOF CHOOF
GOOD HEAVENS! A TRAIN!
S.C.R.R.
31B.
IT'S HEADING NORTH! WHAT A STROKE OF LUCK — WE CAN'T AFFORD TO MISS IT!
NOPE!
SOUTH CAROLINA
54012
SOUTH CAROLINA
54012
WT 19250 LBS
GIVE ME YOUR HAND, HONEY! HURRY!!
DO YOU WANT IT ACROSS YOUR FACE, HUH?!
31B.

PHEW! JUST IN TIME — IT'S PICKING UP SPEED AGAIN!

SOUTH CAROLINA
49500
54012
SOUT CAROL

!

NO TRACE OF ANYONE AROUND HERE, LIEUTENANT!

◎★!俗◎! HOW DID THEY DISGUISE THEMSELVES THIS TIME?!

32A

LIEUTENANT ... OVER HERE!

?

CURSES!

I THINK THEY GOT AWAY FOR GOOD THIS TIME!

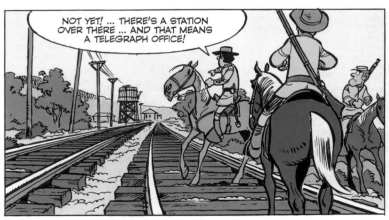
NOT YET! ... THERE'S A STATION OVER THERE ... AND THAT MEANS A TELEGRAPH OFFICE!

AND SOON ...

S.C.R.

TAP TAP

TAP TAP

32B.

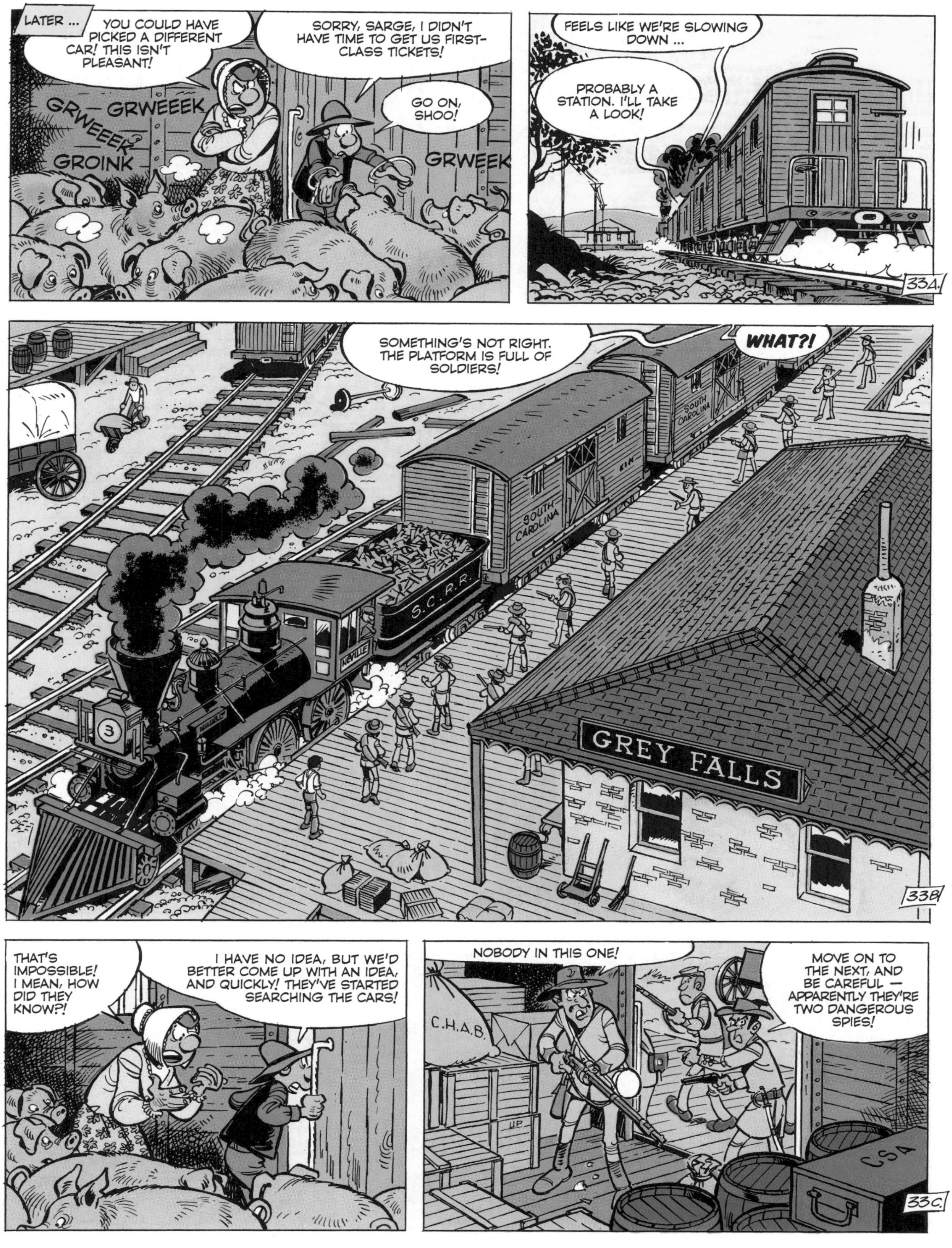
LATER ...
YOU COULD HAVE PICKED A DIFFERENT CAR! THIS ISN'T PLEASANT!
SORRY, SARGE, I DIDN'T HAVE TIME TO GET US FIRST-CLASS TICKETS!
GRWEEEK GRWEEEK
GROINK
GO ON, SHOO!
GRWEEK
FEELS LIKE WE'RE SLOWING DOWN ...
PROBABLY A STATION. I'LL TAKE A LOOK!
33A.
SOMETHING'S NOT RIGHT. THE PLATFORM IS FULL OF SOLDIERS!
WHAT?!
SOUTH CAROLINA
S.C.R.R.
NEVILLE
GREY FALLS
33B
THAT'S IMPOSSIBLE! I MEAN, HOW DID THEY KNOW?!
I HAVE NO IDEA, BUT WE'D BETTER COME UP WITH AN IDEA, AND QUICKLY! THEY'VE STARTED SEARCHING THE CARS!
NOBODY IN THIS ONE!
MOVE ON TO THE NEXT, AND BE CAREFUL — APPARENTLY THEY'RE TWO DANGEROUS SPIES!
C.H.A.B.
CSA
33C.

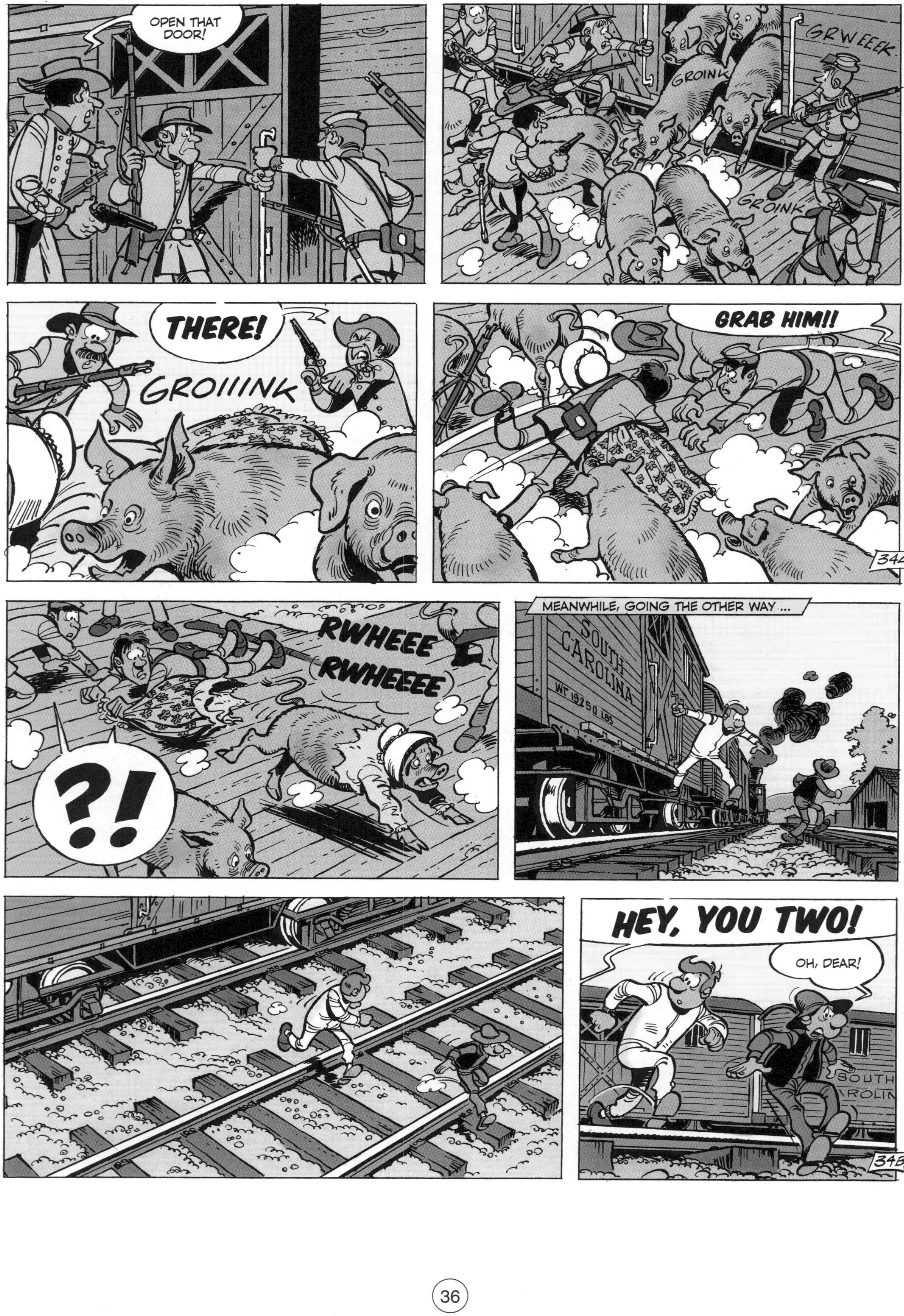

OPEN THAT DOOR!
GRWEEEK
GROINK
GROINK
THERE!
GROIIINK
GRAB HIM!!
34A
RWHEEE
RWHEEEE
?!
MEANWHILE, GOING THE OTHER WAY ...
SOUTH CAROLINA
WT. 19250 LBS
HEY, YOU TWO!
OH, DEAR!
SOUTH
ROLIN
34B

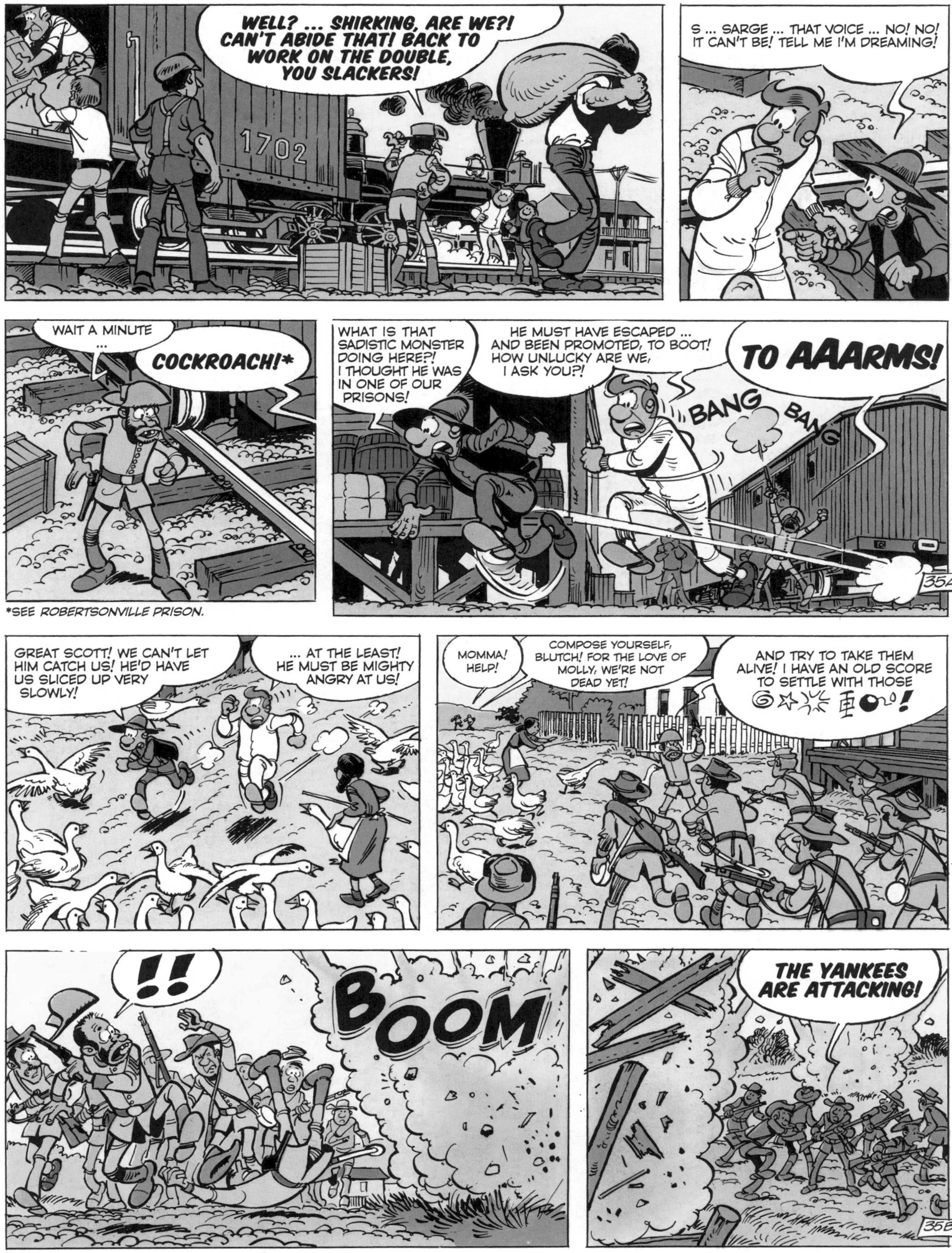
WELL? ... SHIRKING, ARE WE?! CAN'T ABIDE THAT! BACK TO WORK ON THE DOUBLE, YOU SLACKERS!
1702
S ... SARGE ... THAT VOICE ... NO! NO! IT CAN'T BE! TELL ME I'M DREAMING!
WAIT A MINUTE ...
COCKROACH!*
WHAT IS THAT SADISTIC MONSTER DOING HERE?! I THOUGHT HE WAS IN ONE OF OUR PRISONS!
HE MUST HAVE ESCAPED ... AND BEEN PROMOTED, TO BOOT! HOW UNLUCKY ARE WE, I ASK YOU?!
TO AAARMS!
BANG
BANG
35A.
*SEE ROBERTSONVILLE PRISON.
GREAT SCOTT! WE CAN'T LET HIM CATCH US! HE'D HAVE US SLICED UP VERY SLOWLY!
... AT THE LEAST! HE MUST BE MIGHTY ANGRY AT US!
MOMMA! HELP!
COMPOSE YOURSELF, BLUTCH! FOR THE LOVE OF MOLLY, WE'RE NOT DEAD YET!
AND TRY TO TAKE THEM ALIVE! I HAVE AN OLD SCORE TO SETTLE WITH THOSE
!!
BOOM
THE YANKEES ARE ATTACKING!
35B.

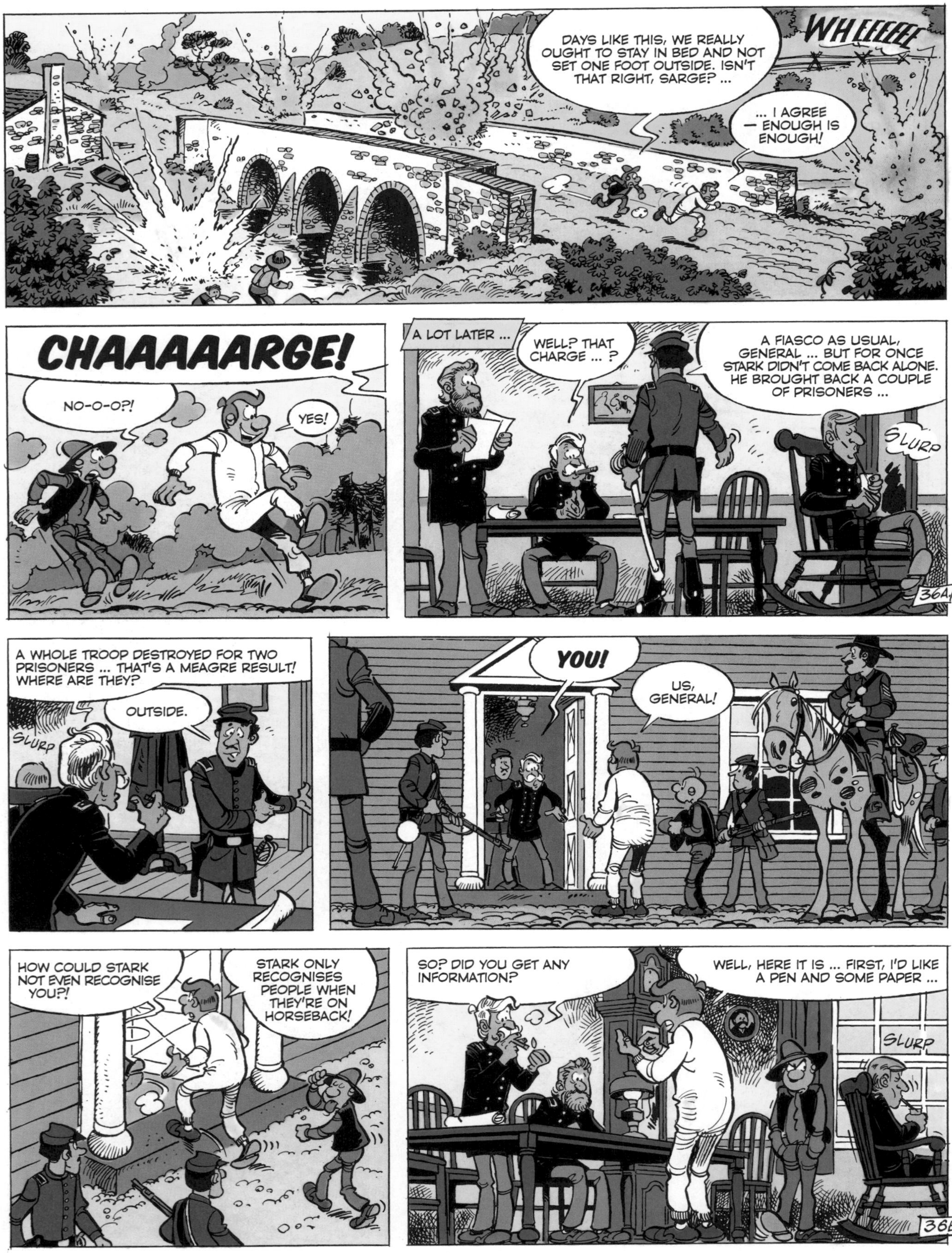

DAYS LIKE THIS, WE REALLY OUGHT TO STAY IN BED AND NOT SET ONE FOOT OUTSIDE. ISN'T THAT RIGHT, SARGE? ...
WHEEEEEE
... I AGREE — ENOUGH IS ENOUGH!
CHAAAAAARGE!
NO-O-O?!
YES!
A LOT LATER ...
WELL? THAT CHARGE ... ?
A FIASCO AS USUAL, GENERAL ... BUT FOR ONCE STARK DIDN'T COME BACK ALONE. HE BROUGHT BACK A COUPLE OF PRISONERS ...
SLURP
36A
A WHOLE TROOP DESTROYED FOR TWO PRISONERS ... THAT'S A MEAGRE RESULT! WHERE ARE THEY?
SLURP
OUTSIDE.
YOU!
US, GENERAL!
HOW COULD STARK NOT EVEN RECOGNISE YOU?!
STARK ONLY RECOGNISES PEOPLE WHEN THEY'RE ON HORSEBACK!
SO? DID YOU GET ANY INFORMATION?
WELL, HERE IT IS ... FIRST, I'D LIKE A PEN AND SOME PAPER ...
SLURP
36B

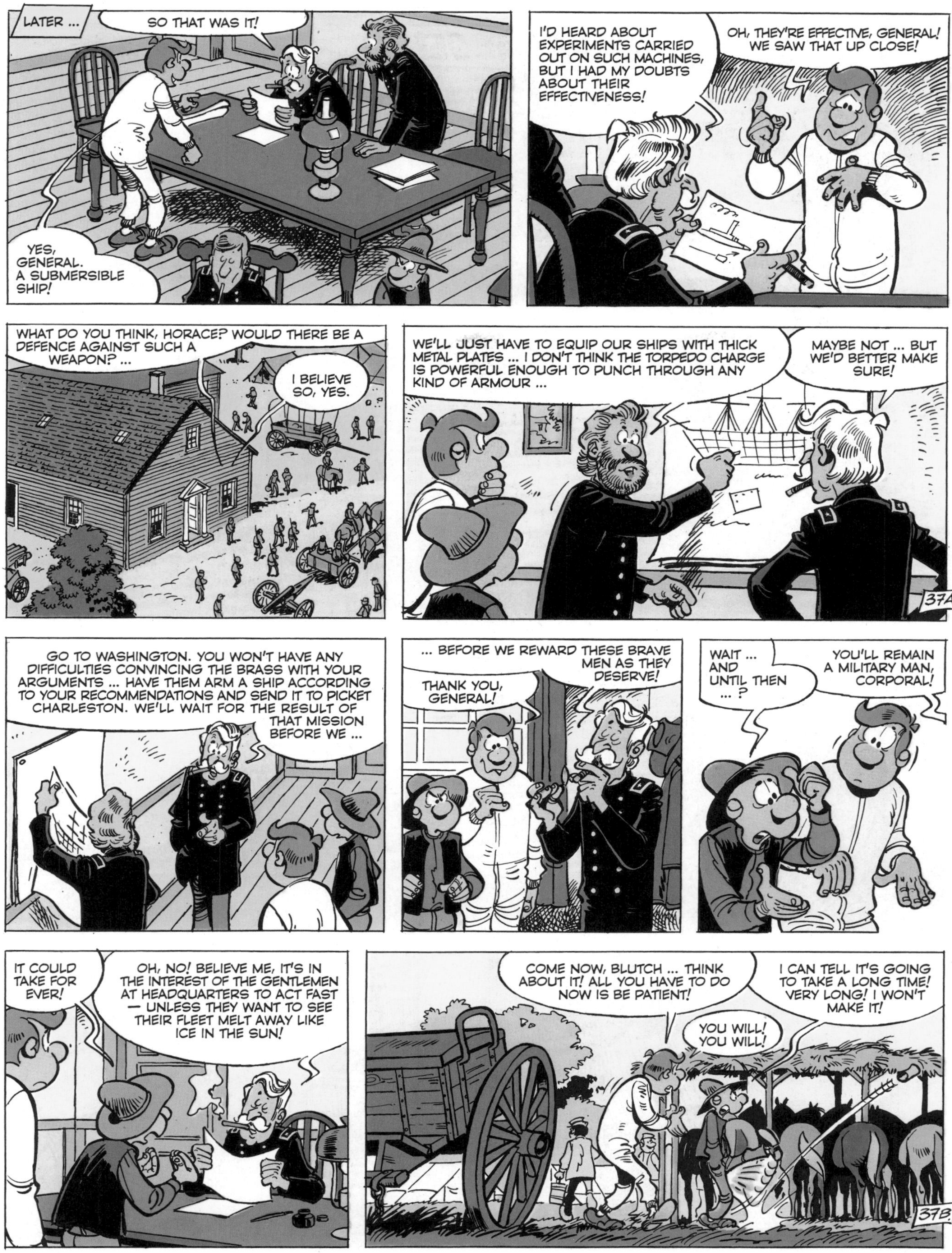
LATER ...
SO THAT WAS IT!
YES, GENERAL. A SUBMERSIBLE SHIP!
I'D HEARD ABOUT EXPERIMENTS CARRIED OUT ON SUCH MACHINES, BUT I HAD MY DOUBTS ABOUT THEIR EFFECTIVENESS!
OH, THEY'RE EFFECTIVE, GENERAL! WE SAW THAT UP CLOSE!
WHAT DO YOU THINK, HORACE? WOULD THERE BE A DEFENCE AGAINST SUCH A WEAPON? ...
I BELIEVE SO, YES.
WE'LL JUST HAVE TO EQUIP OUR SHIPS WITH THICK METAL PLATES ... I DON'T THINK THE TORPEDO CHARGE IS POWERFUL ENOUGH TO PUNCH THROUGH ANY KIND OF ARMOUR ...
MAYBE NOT ... BUT WE'D BETTER MAKE SURE!
37A.
GO TO WASHINGTON. YOU WON'T HAVE ANY DIFFICULTIES CONVINCING THE BRASS WITH YOUR ARGUMENTS ... HAVE THEM ARM A SHIP ACCORDING TO YOUR RECOMMENDATIONS AND SEND IT TO PICKET CHARLESTON. WE'LL WAIT FOR THE RESULT OF THAT MISSION BEFORE WE ...
... BEFORE WE REWARD THESE BRAVE MEN AS THEY DESERVE!
THANK YOU, GENERAL!
WAIT ... AND UNTIL THEN ... ?
YOU'LL REMAIN A MILITARY MAN, CORPORAL!
IT COULD TAKE FOR EVER!
OH, NO! BELIEVE ME, IT'S IN THE INTEREST OF THE GENTLEMEN AT HEADQUARTERS TO ACT FAST — UNLESS THEY WANT TO SEE THEIR FLEET MELT AWAY LIKE ICE IN THE SUN!
COME NOW, BLUTCH ... THINK ABOUT IT! ALL YOU HAVE TO DO NOW IS BE PATIENT!
YOU WILL! YOU WILL!
I CAN TELL IT'S GOING TO TAKE A LONG TIME! VERY LONG! I WON'T MAKE IT!
37B.

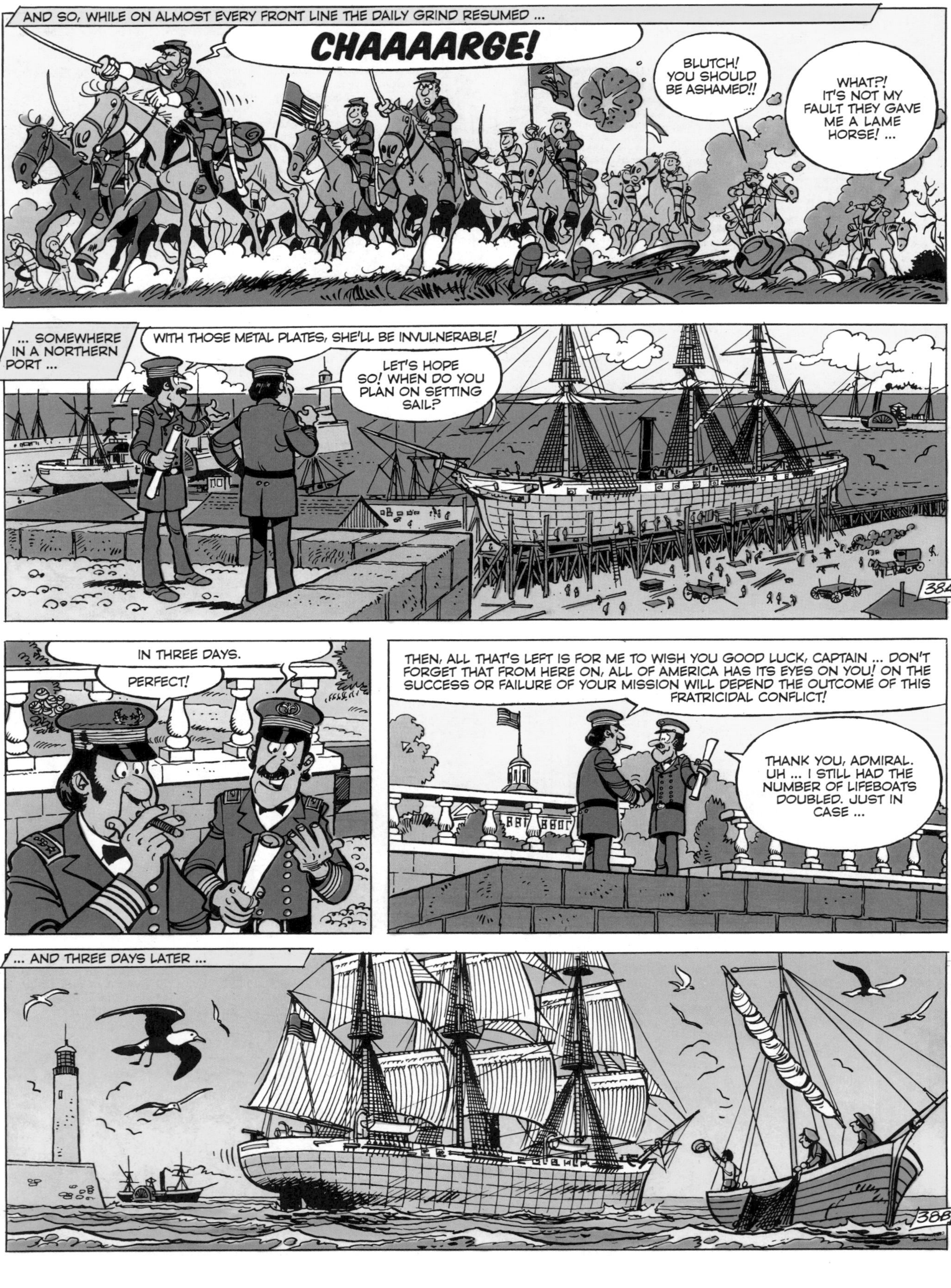
AND SO, WHILE ON ALMOST EVERY FRONT LINE THE DAILY GRIND RESUMED ...
CHAAAARGE!
BLUTCH! YOU SHOULD BE ASHAMED!!
WHAT?! IT'S NOT MY FAULT THEY GAVE ME A LAME HORSE! ...
... SOMEWHERE IN A NORTHERN PORT ...
WITH THOSE METAL PLATES, SHE'LL BE INVULNERABLE!
LET'S HOPE SO! WHEN DO YOU PLAN ON SETTING SAIL?
38A
IN THREE DAYS.
PERFECT!
THEN, ALL THAT'S LEFT IS FOR ME TO WISH YOU GOOD LUCK, CAPTAIN ... DON'T FORGET THAT FROM HERE ON, ALL OF AMERICA HAS ITS EYES ON YOU! ON THE SUCCESS OR FAILURE OF YOUR MISSION WILL DEPEND THE OUTCOME OF THIS FRATRICIDAL CONFLICT!
THANK YOU, ADMIRAL. UH ... I STILL HAD THE NUMBER OF LIFEBOATS DOUBLED. JUST IN CASE ...
... AND THREE DAYS LATER ...
38B

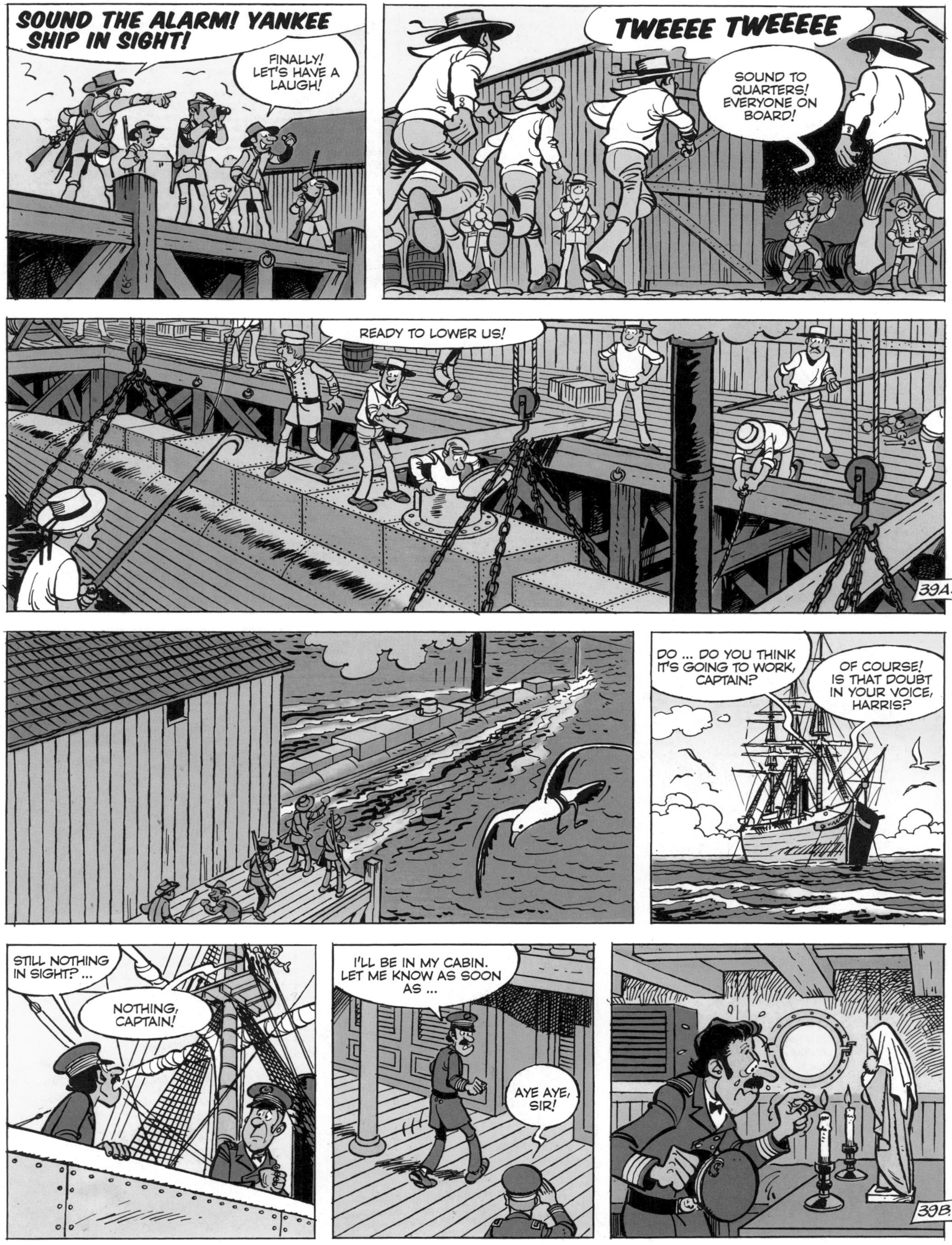
SOUND THE ALARM! YANKEE SHIP IN SIGHT!
FINALLY! LET'S HAVE A LAUGH!
TWEEEE TWEEEEE
SOUND TO QUARTERS! EVERYONE ON BOARD!
READY TO LOWER US!
39A.
DO ... DO YOU THINK IT'S GOING TO WORK, CAPTAIN?
OF COURSE! IS THAT DOUBT IN YOUR VOICE, HARRIS?
STILL NOTHING IN SIGHT? ...
NOTHING, CAPTAIN!
I'LL BE IN MY CABIN. LET ME KNOW AS SOON AS ...
AYE AYE, SIR!
39B.

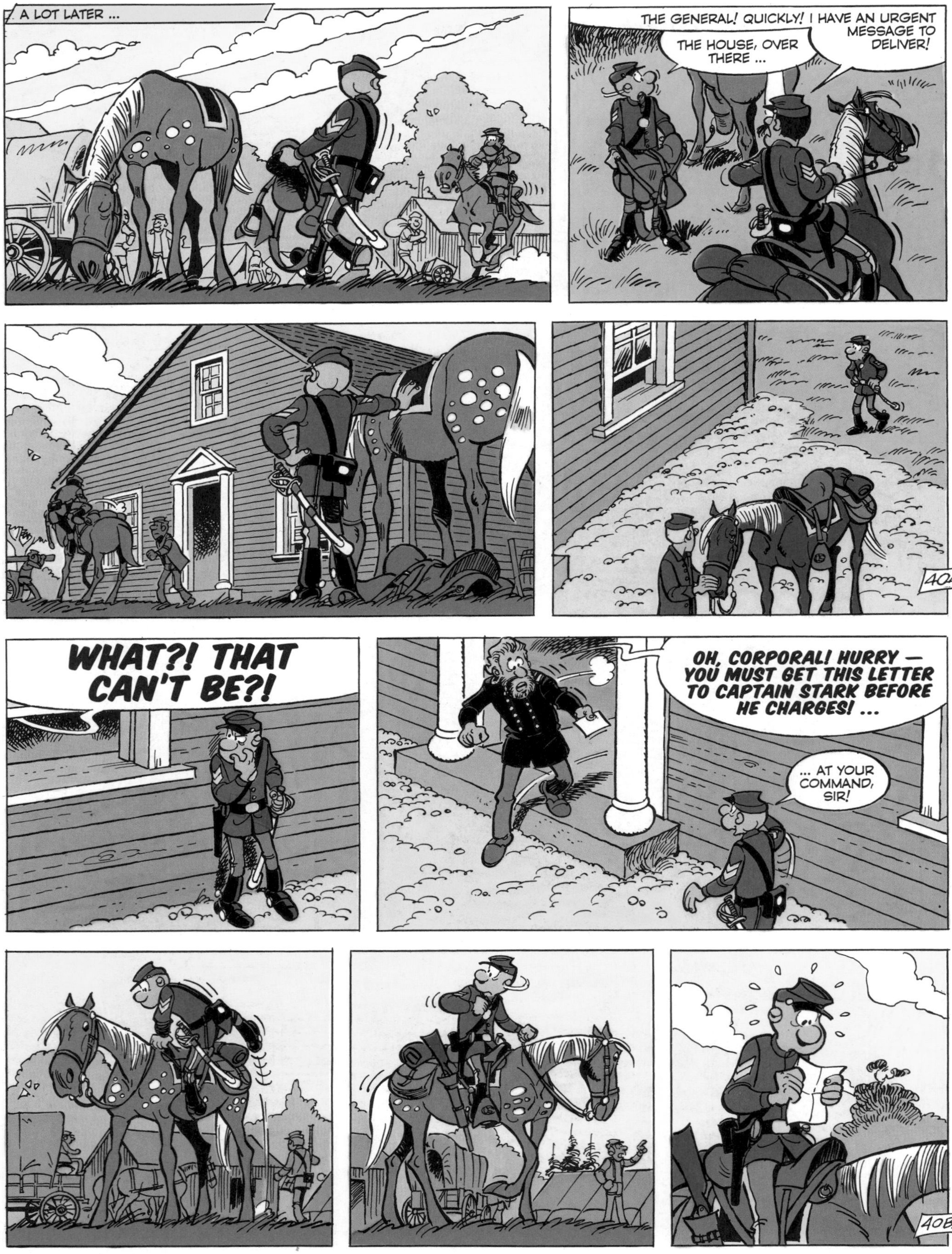
A LOT LATER ...
THE GENERAL! QUICKLY! I HAVE AN URGENT MESSAGE TO DELIVER!
THE HOUSE, OVER THERE ...
40A.
WHAT?! THAT CAN'T BE?!
OH, CORPORAL! HURRY — YOU MUST GET THIS LETTER TO CAPTAIN STARK BEFORE HE CHARGES! ...
... AT YOUR COMMAND, SIR!
40B.

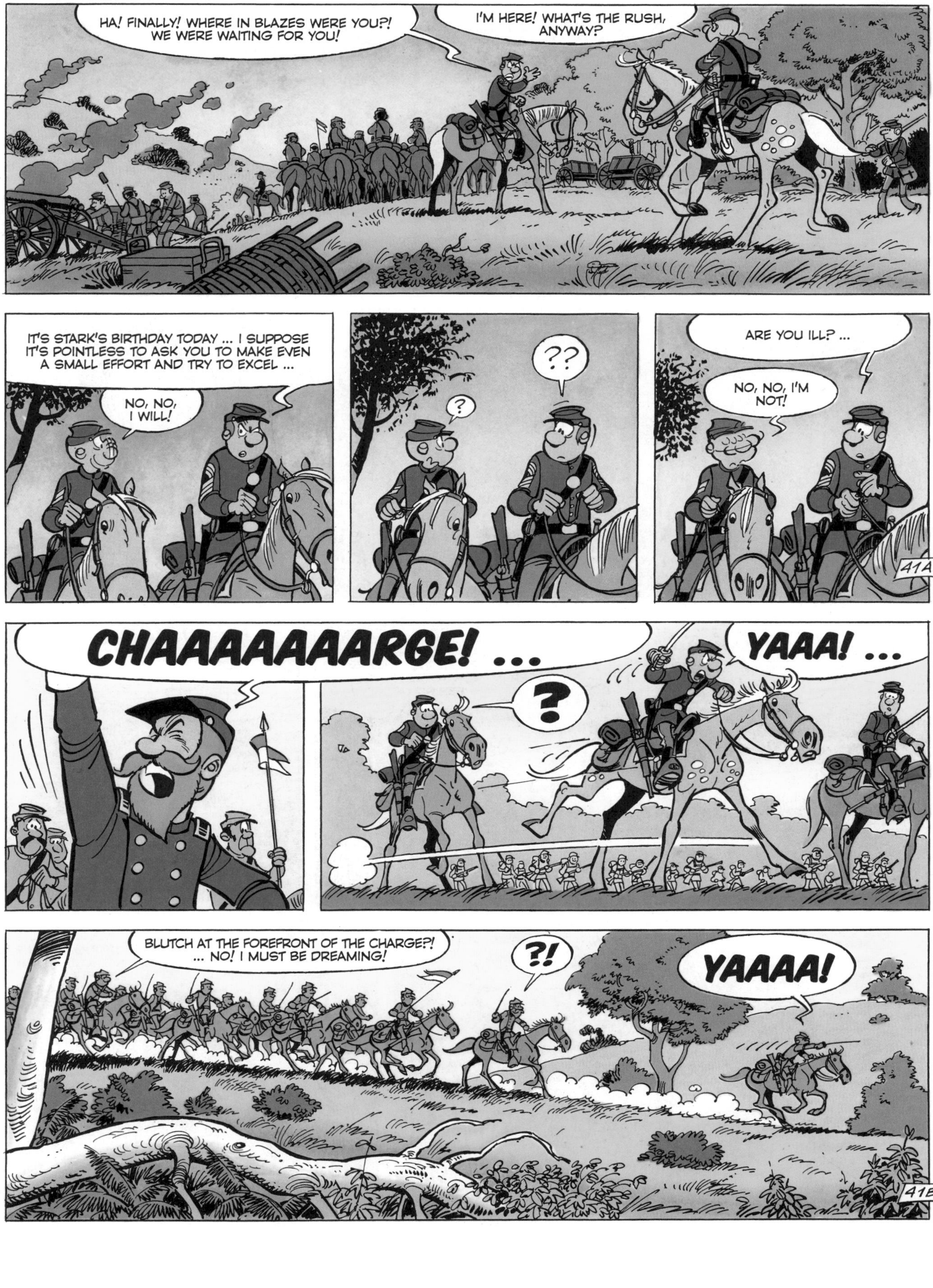

HA! FINALLY! WHERE IN BLAZES WERE YOU?! WE WERE WAITING FOR YOU!
I'M HERE! WHAT'S THE RUSH, ANYWAY?
IT'S STARK'S BIRTHDAY TODAY ... I SUPPOSE IT'S POINTLESS TO ASK YOU TO MAKE EVEN A SMALL EFFORT AND TRY TO EXCEL ...
NO, NO, I WILL!
?
??
ARE YOU ILL? ...
NO, NO, I'M NOT!
41A.
CHAAAAAAAARGE! ...
YAAA! ...
?
BLUTCH AT THE FOREFRONT OF THE CHARGE?! ... NO! I MUST BE DREAMING!
?!
YAAAA!
41B.

LATER ...

GENERAL! WHAT IS GOING ON?! THIS IS INTOLERABLE! ... WE'VE BEEN CHARGING FOR AN HOUR AND WE HAVEN'T MET A SINGLE ENEMY SOLDIER!

WHAT?!

YOU MEAN YOU DIDN'T GET MY MESSAGE?

... MESSAGE? ... WHAT MESSAGE? ...

CORPORAL BLUTCH!

GENERAL? ...

?

42A

THE MESSAGE!

THE ...?! OH, GOODNESS! THE MESSAGE! I'D CLEAN FORGOTTEN ABOUT IT, GENERAL!

IF YOU'D HAD A CHANCE TO READ THIS, CAPTAIN, YOU'D KNOW THAT LAST NIGHT THE CONFEDERATES MANAGED TO MANOEUVRE AROUND OUR POSITIONS. THEY'RE NO LONGER IN FRONT OF US — THEY'RE BEHIND US NOW!

BOOHOOOOO ...

BLUTCH, YOU LITTLE ◎☆⸙!⬙

HEY, WE ALL FORGET THINGS SOMETIMES!

BOOHOOOOO ...

NOW, NOW, CAPTAIN! PULL YOURSELF TOGETHER! A BIG BOY LIKE YOU, REALLY! ...

SOON ...

WELL DONE! YOU CAN BE PROUD OF YOURSELF!

YOU ACTUALLY THOUGHT I WAS GOING TO TAKE ANY RISKS WHEN I'M MERE DAYS FROM A DISCHARGE?! ...

42B

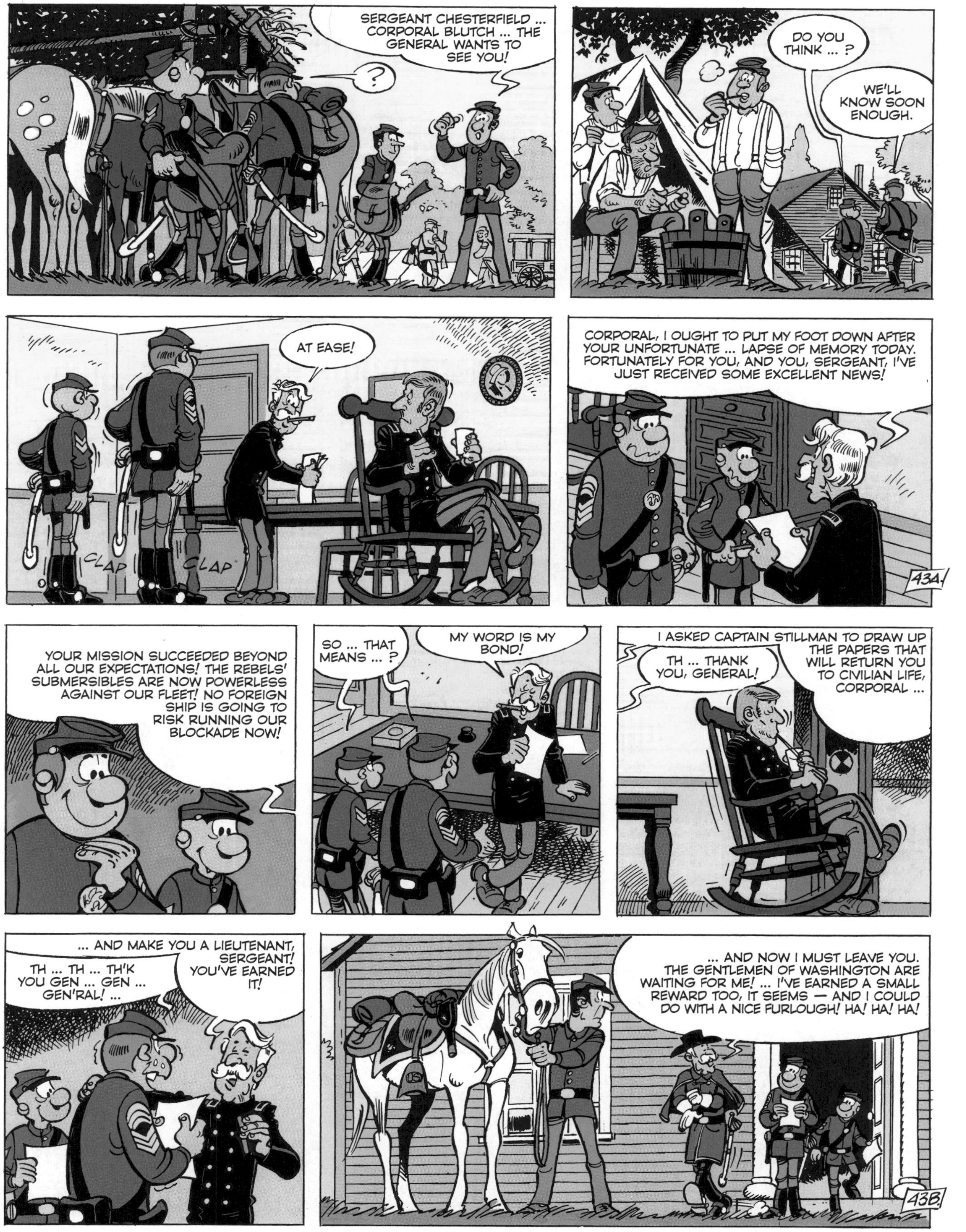
SERGEANT CHESTERFIELD ... CORPORAL BLUTCH ... THE GENERAL WANTS TO SEE YOU!
?
DO YOU THINK ... ?
WE'LL KNOW SOON ENOUGH.
AT EASE!
CLAP
CLAP
CORPORAL, I OUGHT TO PUT MY FOOT DOWN AFTER YOUR UNFORTUNATE ... LAPSE OF MEMORY TODAY. FORTUNATELY FOR YOU, AND YOU, SERGEANT, I'VE JUST RECEIVED SOME EXCELLENT NEWS!
43A
YOUR MISSION SUCCEEDED BEYOND ALL OUR EXPECTATIONS! THE REBELS' SUBMERSIBLES ARE NOW POWERLESS AGAINST OUR FLEET! NO FOREIGN SHIP IS GOING TO RISK RUNNING OUR BLOCKADE NOW!
SO ... THAT MEANS ... ?
MY WORD IS MY BOND!
I ASKED CAPTAIN STILLMAN TO DRAW UP THE PAPERS THAT WILL RETURN YOU TO CIVILIAN LIFE, CORPORAL ...
TH ... THANK YOU, GENERAL!
... AND MAKE YOU A LIEUTENANT, SERGEANT! YOU'VE EARNED IT!
TH ... TH ... TH'K YOU GEN ... GEN ... GEN'RAL! ...
... AND NOW I MUST LEAVE YOU. THE GENTLEMEN OF WASHINGTON ARE WAITING FOR ME! ... I'VE EARNED A SMALL REWARD TOO, IT SEEMS — AND I COULD DO WITH A NICE FURLOUGH! HA! HA! HA!
US
43B

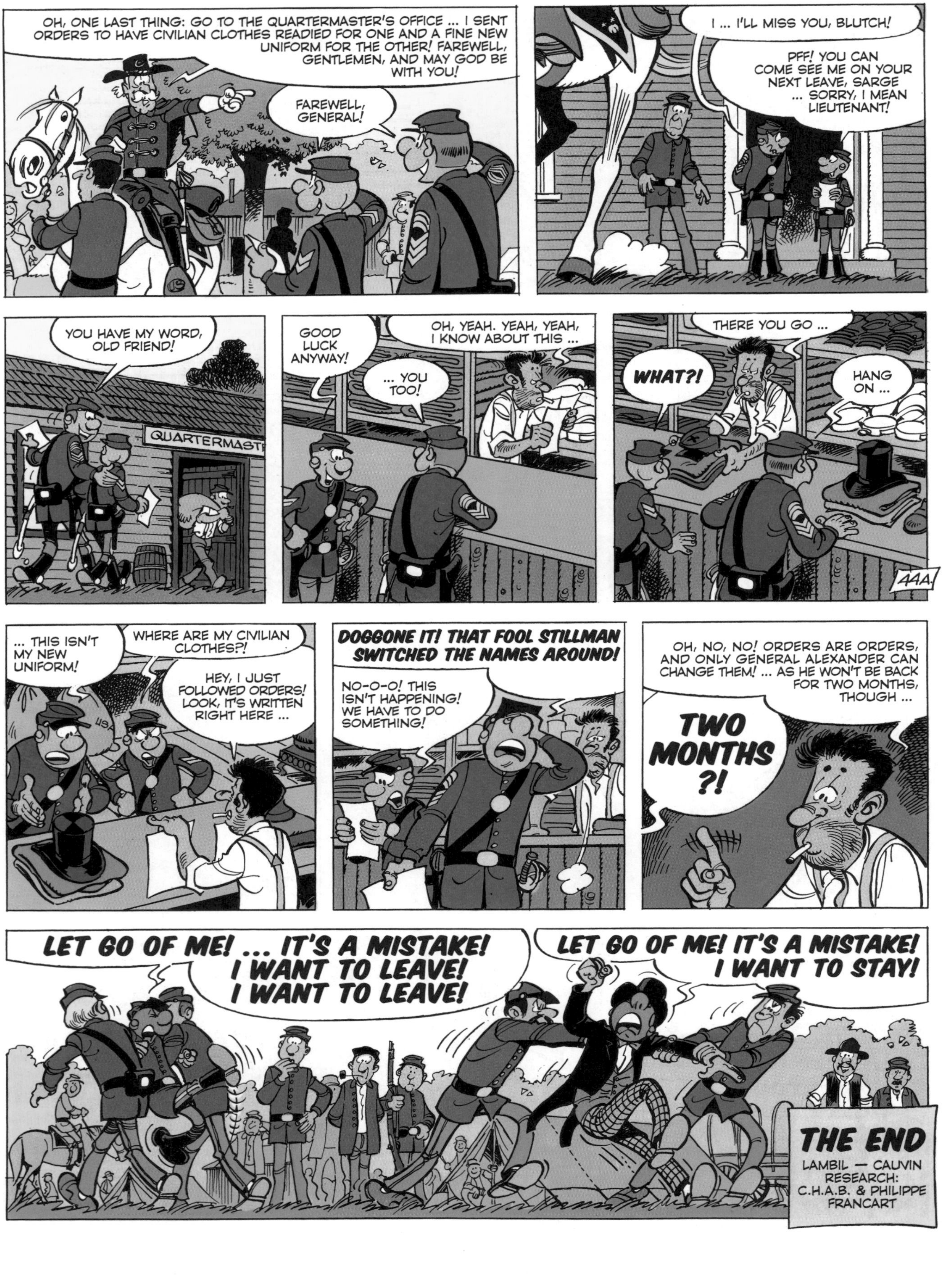
OH, ONE LAST THING: GO TO THE QUARTERMASTER'S OFFICE ... I SENT ORDERS TO HAVE CIVILIAN CLOTHES READIED FOR ONE AND A FINE NEW UNIFORM FOR THE OTHER! FAREWELL, GENTLEMEN, AND MAY GOD BE WITH YOU!
FAREWELL, GENERAL!
I ... I'LL MISS YOU, BLUTCH!
PFF! YOU CAN COME SEE ME ON YOUR NEXT LEAVE, SARGE ... SORRY, I MEAN LIEUTENANT!
YOU HAVE MY WORD, OLD FRIEND!
QUARTERMAST
GOOD LUCK ANYWAY!
... YOU TOO!
OH, YEAH. YEAH, YEAH, I KNOW ABOUT THIS ...
THERE YOU GO ...
WHAT?!
HANG ON ...
AAA!
... THIS ISN'T MY NEW UNIFORM!
WHERE ARE MY CIVILIAN CLOTHES?!
HEY, I JUST FOLLOWED ORDERS! LOOK, IT'S WRITTEN RIGHT HERE ...
DOGGONE IT! THAT FOOL STILLMAN SWITCHED THE NAMES AROUND!
NO-O-O! THIS ISN'T HAPPENING! WE HAVE TO DO SOMETHING!
OH, NO, NO! ORDERS ARE ORDERS, AND ONLY GENERAL ALEXANDER CAN CHANGE THEM! ... AS HE WON'T BE BACK FOR TWO MONTHS, THOUGH ...
TWO MONTHS ?!
LET GO OF ME! ... IT'S A MISTAKE! I WANT TO LEAVE! I WANT TO LEAVE!
LET GO OF ME! IT'S A MISTAKE! I WANT TO STAY!
THE END
LAMBIL — CAUVIN
RESEARCH: C.H.A.B. & PHILIPPE FRANCART

THE BLUECOATS

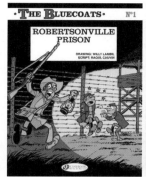

THE BLUECOATS N°1
ROBERTSONVILLE PRISON
DRAWING: WILLY LAMBIL
SCRIPT: RAOUL CAUVIN
1 - ROBERTSONVILLE PRISON

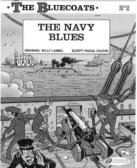

THE BLUECOATS N°2
THE NAVY BLUES
DRAWING: WILLY LAMBIL SCRIPT: RAOUL CAUVIN
2 - THE NAVY BLUES

THE BLUECOATS N°3
THE SKYRIDERS
DRAWING: WILLY LAMBIL SCRIPT: RAOUL CAUVIN
3 - THE SKYRIDERS

THE BLUECOATS N°4
THE GREENHORN
DRAWING: WILLY LAMBIL SCRIPT: RAOUL CAUVIN
4 - THE GREENHORN

THE BLUECOATS N°5
RUMBERLEY
DRAWING: WILLY LAMBIL SCRIPT: RAOUL CAUVIN
5 - RUMBERLEY

THE BLUECOATS N°6
BRONCO BENNY
DRAWING: WILLY LAMBIL
SCRIPT: RAOUL CAUVIN
6 - BRONCO BENNY

THE BLUECOATS N°7
THE BLUES IN THE MUD
DRAWING: WILLY LAMBIL SCRIPT: RAOUL CAUVIN
7 - THE BLUES IN THE MUD

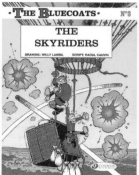

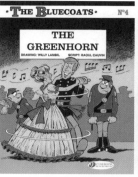

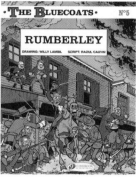

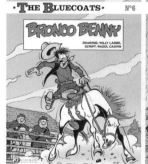

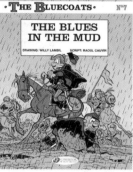

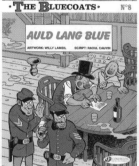

THE BLUECOATS N°8
AULD LANG BLUE
ARTWORK: WILLY LAMBIL SCRIPT: RAOUL CAUVIN
8 - AULD LANG BLUE

THE BLUECOATS N°9
EL PADRE
ARTWORK: WILLY LAMBIL
SCRIPT: RAOUL CAUVIN
9 - EL PADRE

THE BLUECOATS N°10
THE BLUES IN BLACK AND WHITE
ARTWORK: WILLY LAMBIL SCRIPT: RAOUL CAUVIN
10 - THE BLUES IN BLACK AND WHITE

COMING SOON

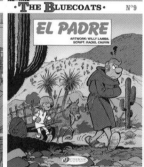

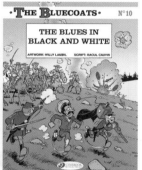

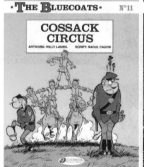

THE BLUECOATS N°11
COSSACK CIRCUS
ARTWORK: WILLY LAMBIL SCRIPT: RAOUL CAUVIN
11 - COSSACK CIRCUS

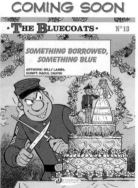

THE BLUECOATS N°12
THE DAVID
ARTWORK: WILLY LAMBIL SCRIPT: RAOUL CAUVIN
12 - THE *DAVID*

THE BLUECOATS N°13
SOMETHING BORROWED, SOMETHING BLUE
ARTWORK: WILLY LAMBIL
SCRIPT: RAOUL CAUVIN
13 - SOMETHING BORROWED, SOMETHING BLUE

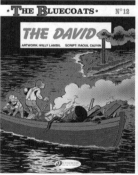

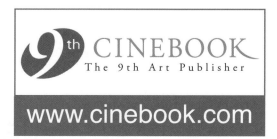

9th CINEBOOK
The 9th Art Publisher
www.cinebook.com